I am Minded to Rise

The Clothing, Weapons and Accoutrements of the Jacobites in Scotland 1689–1719

Jenn Scott

Helion & Company

Helion & Company Limited
Unit 8 Amherst Business Centre
Budbrooke Road
Warwick
CV34 5WE
England
Tel. 01926 499 619
Email: info@helion.co.uk
Website: www.helion.co.uk
Twitter: @helionbooks
Blog: blog.helion.co.uk

Published by Helion & Company 2020
Designed and typeset by Mach 3 Solutions Ltd (www.mach3solutions.co.uk)
Cover designed by Paul Hewitt, Battlefield Design (www.battlefield-design.co.uk)

Text © Jenn Scott 2020
Illustrations © as individually credited
Colour artwork drawn by Seán Ó Brógain © Helion & Company 2020
Colour flags drawn by Mark Allen © Helion & Company 2020

ISBN 978-1-912866-63-2

British Library Cataloguing-in-Publication Data.
A catalogue record for this book is available from the British Library.

For details of other military history titles published by Helion & Company Limited
contact the above address or visit our website: http://www.helion.co.uk.

We always welcome receiving book proposals from prospective authors.

For Kit

A bright and brave, shining star

Contents

Lists of Illustrations

Acknowledgements

I would like to thank all of the people who have given generously of their time and expertise while I have been writing this; found me articles, answered my odd queries and generally helped me to think that I could write another book. In particular, I would like to thank my editor, Charles Singleton and Helion & Company; the Stewart Society for allowing me to use their library once more; Seán Ó Brógain for his lovely pictures which bring the people vividly to life; Elizabeth Quarmby-Lawrence for all her assistance with the more obscure articles; Dave Roberts and Alison Rodham who a very long time ago inspired my interest in the 18th century, Dr Arran Johnston for allowing me to bounce ideas off him, Sean Chamberlain for his enthusiastic support and as ever my mum, Frances Scott.

Jenn Scott
Edinburgh, December 2019

Introduction

Och, s mis' 'th' air mo chlisgeadh,
Saoir bhith sabhadh do chiste,
'Sgun do chaireadh fo lic thu,
An aite falaich gun fhios duinn..
Si a' bhlaidha thug sgrios oirnn!
S' daor a phlaigh sinn air sibht Mhorair Marr sin

(Och I am distraught
At carpenters sawing your coffin
At your being laid under a slab
In some hidden place we don't know.
Oh how this year has ruined us!
We paid dear for that plan of Lord Mar's)[1]

This book covers quite a large amount of time: from the very beginning of Jacobite period in 1689 and Killiecrankie, which is perhaps the battle that looks most like the popular image of Jacobite battles, complete with Lochaber axes, the Highland charge and half naked Highlanders sword in hand, to the often forgotten battle of Glenshiel in 1719 which with the involvement of uniformed Spanish regulars and defensive fighting with the heavy use of guns was completely different. The clothing, weapons and accoutrements of those who 'came out' for the Stuarts in Scotland during this time changed greatly and thus tells us a considerable amount, not just about them, but about their politics and the material culture of the Jacobites and Scotland as a whole.

By landing in the south-west of England in 1688, William of Orange set in motion a century of political unrest. James VII and II after he fled to France, and his descendants, James VIII and III and famously Charles Edward Stuart, spent all those years in various plots to reclaim the throne. Their supporters, known as Jacobites after 'Jacobus', the Latin for James, came from across the social classes; the aristocracy to the underworld. In this book

---

1   Gaor nam Ban Muileach Mairerad nighean Lachlainn (Margaret MacLean)

I intend to look at some of those supporters in Scotland, what they wore, fought with and some of what they carried with them.

Throughout the book I have tried to call anyone I refer to by their contemporary titles unless that makes it just too confusing. However, I have made the deliberate decision to call King James VII and II and his descendants by those titles and not anything else. I have generally kept to original spellings in any quotations and put any translations in brackets after Gaelic and French. I have also kept to original names for items of clothing except where using them would cause some confusion. The two sides, I refer to as Jacobite and the British or Government army.

Timeline of the Risings in Scotland

1685

James VII and II became King. James VII was a Catholic. Risings led by the Duke of Argyll in Scotland and the Duke of Monmouth in England – with the aim of putting Protestant Monmouth, the illegitimate son of Charles II, on the throne – failed.

In Scotland, the King's supporters in Parliament had attempted to force the Covenanters (Presbyterians) to give up their faith and accept the Episcopalian Church.

1688

10 June: The King's son, James, was born. The birth of a Catholic heir who would depose his Protestant sister, Princess Mary, led to approaches being made by the Protestant Lords to Mary's husband William, Prince of Orange.

5 November: Prince William of Orange landed at Torbay with the Dutch army of 14,000. Many men and officers defected to William of Orange which caused both the English Army and James VII and II to become increasingly demoralised.

10 December: The Queen escaped to France with the Prince of Wales; James ordered the English Army to disband, threw the Great Seal into the Thames, fled London, and two weeks later escaped to France.

1689

28 January: Parliament declared that James had abdicated his throne by fleeing.

13 February: William and Mary proclaimed as joint sovereigns of England.

12 March: King James landed in Ireland with 5,000 French troops.

25 March: William and Mary were proclaimed joint sovereigns of Scotland by the Scottish Convention.

18 May: John Graham of Claverhouse, Viscount Dundee mustered the Jacobite clans in support of King James at Lochaber.

17 July: Dundee won the battle of Killiecrankie against the Williamite forces led by Major General Mackay, but Dundee was killed. This was a major setback for the Jacobites.

21 August: Major General Cannon's Jacobite army was defeated by Lieutenant Colonel Cleland at Dunkeld.

1690

1 May: Major General Buchan and the Jacobite army were routed at the Haughs of Cromdale. Guerrilla warfare began in the Highlands.

7 June: Presbyterianism was officially re-established in Scotland.

12 July: King James defeated at the Battle of the Boyne by King William. James left Ireland for France and exile.

1691

30 June: The Earl of Breadalbane negotiated a truce in the Highland war while the Jacobites sought King James's permission to surrender.

3 October: Limerick surrendered. The remnant of the Irish Jacobite army (around 14,000), many with their wives and children, was evacuated to France in what is known as the flight of the Wild Geese.

2 December: James gave the Jacobite clans his permission to surrender.

1692

January: Jacobite clans surrendered.

13 January: the Massacre of the MacDonalds of Glencoe took place.

19–20 May: an Anglo-Dutch fleet under Admiral Russell chased away the French fleet and burned ships at La Hogue. Consequently the plan of a French-supported Jacobite invasion was abandoned.

1694

18 April: The last Jacobite refuge, the Bass Rock in the Firth of Forth, surrendered.

28 December: Queen Mary died.

1697

10 September: Louis XIV recognised William as King of the Three Kingdoms. James turned down King William's offer to acknowledge James Edward Stuart as his heir, since he would have had to have been raised as a Protestant.

1701

24 April: An Act of Succession nominated the House of Hanover as William and Princess Anne's heirs. This meant that Sophia, Electress of Hanover, a granddaughter of James VI, would inherit the throne if King William and then Princess Anne died without heirs.

September: Italy began the War of the Spanish Succession.

6 September: Death of James VII and II. Louis XIV recognised the Prince of Wales as James VIII and III.

1702

8 March: Death of William. Queen Anne acceded to the throne.

15 May: England, Scotland and Ireland declared war on France and Spain.

1707

1 May: The Act of Union between Scotland and England came into force.

October: The French king ordered that the Enterprise of Scotland could begin. The plan was to land approximately 5,000 troops in Scotland whereupon there would be a popular rising, which would if all went as planned, drive Government troops out of Scotland.

1708

27 February: James Edward arrived in Dunkirk hoping to begin invasion of Scotland, however he was ill with measles. A Royal Navy squadron commanded by Admiral Byng arrived off Dunkirk.

6 March: The French invasion fleet evaded Byng's ships and sailed for Scotland.

12 March: The French fleet arrived in the Firth of Forth too late to land that day. However, the next day Byng's fleet was sighted, and the French fleet, commanded by Comte de Forbin, fled north. When he was unable to land in Inverness due to the wind, he decided to return to Dunkirk.

1714

1 August: Queen Anne died. George I declared king.

1715

9 August: Earl of Marl left London for Scotland, arrived 16 August, and went to the Highlands.

21 August: Death of Louis XIV; Duke of Orleans became Regent.

6 September: The raising of the Jacobite standard by Mar, at Braemar.

8 September: Thomas Arthur led unsuccessful raid on Edinburgh Castle.

17 September: Perth captured by Hay of Cromlix for the Jacobites. Mar established Jacobite HQ there.

11 October: Viscount Kenmuir mustered the Borderers for the Jacobites at Moffat.

12–13 October: Macintosh of Borlum and his men crossed the Firth of Forth.

17 October: James set out for the French coast, arriving at St Malo at the end of the month.

22 October: Borlum joined the Borderers.

6 November: James attempted to leave the country but was driven back due to bad weather.

12 November: Mar marched south from Perth towards Dunblane. The Duke of Argyll advanced from Stirling to Sheriffmuir.

13 November: Mar and Argyll fought at Sheriffmuir.

14 November: Perth retreated to Perth.

16 December: James embarked at Dunkirk.

22 December: James landed at Peterhead, near Aberdeen.

1716

31 January: James retreated from Perth, since Argyll had advanced north.

4 February: James and Mar sailed from Montrose for France.

1718

October: Preparations for a Spanish invasion of England began.

6 December: Britain declared war on Spain.

1719

27 January: James left for Spain.

24 February: Spanish invasion force left for England. Diversionary Spanish invasion force left for Scotland under Earl Marischal.

18 March: The main Spanish expedition was dispersed by bad weather and therefore the planned invasion of England was abandoned.

9 April: Earl Marischal and two ships reached Lewis.

10 June: Earl Marischal and his army were defeated at Glenshiel by Major General Wightman.[1]

---

1   D. Szechi, *The Jacobites, Britain and Europe, 1688–1788* (Manchester: Manchester University Press, 2019), pp.xv–xxvi.

1

The Time of Sword Unsheathing

'n iam rusgadh nan lann
Is an am nam builleanan,
Tha mi am chadal,
Ged tha sibh san iam
Feadh ghleann is mhunaidhean:
Gun tog sibh bhur ceann
'n iam teanndachd mar churaidhean:
gun tig Seamus-a-nall,
'sbhurr lann a bhios fuileachdach
(In the time of sword-unsheathing,
And in time of blow-striking,
I am asleep, don't wake me up,
Though now you are scattered,
Among the glens and the hills
You will rise again
When it is time for you once more to be heroes,
Until James comes across,
And your swords become bloodied)[1]

From the end of the sixteenth century in Scotland, the government of James VI attempted to bring greater political and administrative order to the Highlands, somewhere that the Scots crown had not been able to exercise the same amount of control as the rest of Scotland partially because of the clan system, the historic dominance of the Lordship of the Isles on the West coast and the geography which made large areas less accessible by land.[2] The Government sought to use many of the same tactics which it had found

---

1   Tha mi am chadal, nadûisgibh mi, Sileasna Ceapaich (Julia MacDonald).
2   S. Stroh, 'The Modern Nation-State and Its Others: Civilizing Missions at Home and Abroad, Ca. 1600 to 1800', in *Gaelic Scotland in the Colonial Imagination: Anglophone Writing from 1600 to 1900*, 33–76 (Northwestern University Press, 2017), p.59. See also Devine, T.M. Devine, *The Scottish Clearances: A History of the Dispossessed* (London: Penguin, 2018), pp.26–29.

successful previously in pacifying the Borders. So, therefore, with the Statutes of Iona in 1609, the government attempted to bring the Highland chiefs and with them the clans under some sort of control, wanting in effect to civilise them by making their way of life more like that of the rest of Scotland. Clauses 3 and 7 of the Statutes of Iona required the chiefs' military retinues to be limited and the carrying of firearms to be suppressed. Importantly for the scope of this book, thus implying that there were already enough guns in the Highlands to be worth controlling. These measures were clearly aimed at breaking the ability of chiefs to command large numbers of fighting men, 'their fighting tails' and to encourage a distance between the chiefs and the people, whom they had always regarded as not only the source of their power but their responsibility. However, since in the Highlands the 1600s were a time of almost continuous warfare, this attempt to bring the region under central control, was less than successful. Some historians have claimed that by the latter part of the seventeenth century the Highlands were growing quieter and while this was true to some degree, the Argyll rebellion took place in 1685, the last clan battle in 1688, and of course the first Jacobite Rising in 1689 and subsequently the massacre of Glencoe in 1692.

In the period with which this book is concerned, Highland society was in transition, with many chiefs and landowners beginning to move away from a traditional way of life which was essentially destroyed post Culloden; nonetheless at this time the social structure of the clan was still in place. The chief (*ceanncinnidh* – literally the head of the kindred) was the head of the clan and he was in a mutual relationship with the clan gentry (*daoine-uaisle* – the noble people) and the tacksmen (*fear-tacsa*). Sometimes these were the same people but not always.

Under these chiefs were several gentlemen of the name who had again under them their tenants and vassals, 'the first are their absolute slaves … they will come together arm'd in a moment ready for any mischief that the Laird shall command them to do',[3] as a Whig pamphleteer described the relationship. In reality the tacksmen leased large tracts of land from the clan chief, and in return frequently they owed the chief man rent, that is they were expected to provide a certain number of men in the case of war. They farmed some of the land and then sub-let the rest to plebeian tenants (*tuathanach*) who paid the rent in a mixture of money, goods and services. In general, the tacksmen could not easily evict tenants and the tenants could not leave very simply to look for better employment, nor at this time would anyone have wanted them to do so. This closer relationship than the landowners in the south meant that chiefs were still able to call upon large numbers of men to form a military retinue in times of conflict to fight in a way that magnates in the Lowlands or England simply could not hope to do by the late 1600s. Although at that time their tenants would still consider themselves to have owed some loyalty to the local landowner, and he to them. Although this kin-

---

3   Anon., *An Historical account of the Highlanders: describing their country, division into clans … set forth in a view of the rebellion in Scotland* (Dublin, 1715), p.12. The Whigs did not want a Catholic monarch, saw themselves as the enemies of absolutism and therefore were resolutely anti-Jacobite.

based society was not unique to the highlands, the families of the Borders had been very similar, however it persisted in the Highlands for longer very largely because of the strength of Gaelic culture and the sheer geographic difficulties of imposing the state authority. The relationship between the chief and those who lived in the district was however still a powerful one, as can be seen in the loyalty of some tenants after the forfeiture of estates which occurred 1715 and 1745. For example, after the '15, the Earl of Seaforth's tenants continued to support him including financially.[4]

The Jacobite cause was for some a lifetime's commitment that was subsequently passed on to their sons, but 'it need not be assumed that all Jacobites maintained an unflagging, lifelong devotion to the Stuart family'.[5] There were also those, like the Earl of Mar, who had been brought later to Jacobitism by disenchantment with the regime, their hopes for religious freedom, or dislike of the Union with England.

The number of men that Viscount Dundee was able to raise in 1689 in support of the House of Stuart was not that great, probably around 2,600, far fewer than the numbers in the field in the later Rising of 1715.[6] Although eventually some 4,000 or so men were involved, including approximately 300 horse, more than the 50 horse who had stayed loyal as Dundee rode out of Edinburgh in April 1689. Crucially, he was unable to access the men from the later Jacobite heartland of the north-east of Scotland. The majority of his men came instead from the western clans, and the Duke of Hamilton's fears in 1689 that Dundee would be 'master of all the other side of the Forth where they are so great numbers disaffected to join him' never materialised.[7] This meant that Dundee's army was made up mostly of Highland men bolstered by some raw Irish troops. In contrast, Daniel Szechi estimates that there were as perhaps as many as 21,000 men in total involved in the '15, although it should be said that were actually probably no more than 15,000 men in arms at any one time.[8]

The very largely Highland nature of the first Rising had a number of consequences. An idea developed that Jacobitism was politically backward and reliant on the 'barbarous' clans – it could be argued that this is an idea that is still held by many, and not helped by recent portrayals of the Risings on TV or in books. This idea was designed to demonstrate that the Jacobites were largely Gaelic, Highland, and therefore uncivilised. There were also more immediate results. Some clans were now seen as enemies of the state. It was this hostility that contributed to the massacre of MacDonalds of Glencoe, including their chief, MacIain, in February 1692.

4   H. Cheape and I.F. Grant, 'Periods In Highland History', 3rd edition (New York: Barnes & Noble, 2000), p.145.

5   P. Monod, *Jacobitism and the English People 1688–1788* (Cambridge: Cambridge University Press, 1993), p.4.

6   M. Pittock, *The Myth of the Jacobite Clans*, (Edinburgh: Edinburgh University Press, 2015), pp.45–6.

7   J. Mackay and Bannatyne Club, *The Life of Lieut.-General Hugh Mackay of Scoury, Commander in Chief of the Forces in Scotland, 1689 and 1690...* (Edinburgh: Laing and Forbes, 1836), p.147.

8   Pittock, *The Myth of the Jacobite Clans*, p.55.

While the gentry in the Lowlands no longer had the ability to summon their tenants to war in the way that their ancestors had a century before, the deep religious divisions that existed in Scotland in the seventeenth century meant that ordinary Lowlanders were more prepared to fight in support of those who shared their beliefs than the majority of common men elsewhere in Britain. The divide between the Covenanters and the Episcopalians became more acute in 1689 when the Episcopalian bishops decided that they must stay loyal to James VII and II as the anointed king. Therefore, they refused to acknowledge King William. This meant that many of those Episcopalian clergy were thrown out of their parishes or were at least under threat of being so. According to Edmund Burt in his *Letters from the North of Scotland*, written in the 1720s and 1730s, the clergy were 'teaching them, that it is as unchristian not to believe their notions of government as to believe the gospel'.[9] The strongest Jacobite areas in the eighteenth century were Episcopalian. For example, in Aberdeenshire and Moray almost half of the people were Episcopalian. The idea that the Jacobites were all Catholic was part of contemporary anti-Jacobite propaganda, so great was the fear that the Catholics might act as some kind of fifth column to bring back 'Papist' ways. It was also further proof for many contemporaries that the Highlanders were 'uncivilised'. In 1703, the Glasgow and Ayr Synod wrote: 'While they continue in their present neglected state Strangers to the Gospell and bound up to a separate language and interest of their own, they are most dangerous to this church and nation, ready to assist invading Forrainners or to break out for plunder in case of Domestick troubles.'[10] However, it is true that Scots Catholics were at this period committed to the Jacobite cause in disproportionate numbers and many remained loyal even after the '45.

On James's death in 1701, the Act of Settlement excluded all Catholic heirs from the English crown and Sophia of Hanover became the heir to Queen Anne. As a Protestant granddaughter of James VI and I she became heir presumptive to the crowns of England and Ireland.[11] The Scottish Parliament's reluctance to pass a similar act was one of the factors that brought about the Union in 1707, although after 1707 Sophia became the heir in Scotland. The Union of the Parliaments increased support for Jacobitism beyond the Episcopalian and Highland heartlands. After the Union, there were many pro-Jacobite demonstrations throughout Scotland, particularly in Edinburgh. The Scottish economy was also still weak, and taxation – described by many as 'tribute money' – had increased considerably as a result of the union.[12] The suffering of the ill years of the 1690s, where up to 13 percent of the population died or emigrated after successive years of poor harvests, had also contributed to an increase in Jacobite sympathy, but

9   E. Burt, ed. A. Simmons, *Burt's Letters from the North of Scotland* (Edinburgh: Birlinn, 1998. First published 1754), p.224.
10 Stroh, 'The Modern Nation-State and Its Others', p.67.
11 She died less than two months before she would have become queen, and succeeded her cousin Anne. Her claim to the throne passed on to her eldest son, George, Elector of Hanover, who ruled as George I.
12 Pittock, *The Myth of the Jacobite Clans*, p.145.

probably also resulted in reduction in violence in the Highlands.[13] Some Episcopalian clergy had suggested that the famine was a punishment for abandoning the Stuarts. Szechi says that the Episcopalian clergy were 'so imbued with a bitter Jacobitism that it would take the better part of a century to persuade them to think again about their support for the house of Stuart'.[14]

Although the conquest of Gaelic Ireland at the start of seventeenth century had removed the opportunity for Highlanders to work as mercenaries in Ireland there remained opportunities in Europe. Therefore, Highland men, despite the relative quietness of the Highlands by the early eighteenth century, often had military experience from fighting abroad in other European armies, if not at home. It was the clan gentlemen and tacksmen who had held command rank in the European military that explain why it was possible to create clan regiments, that used their own clansmen as officers, during the later Jacobite risings. The clan gentlemen were the best armed fighters, generally with a long gun, a pair of pistols, a dirk and a sword. 'You seldom see them, though only taking air, without a sword and a dirk, sometimes called a skene[15] and which is a short dagger, now they carry muskets and other firearms.'[16] Thomas Kirke in *A Modern Account of Scotland* written in 1679 claimed that the Highlanders put poison on their dirks which were about a 'foot or half a yard long.'[17] They fought in the front rank in any battle and led from the front. They were expected to help uphold order, and if necessary guard clan lands from possible attack.[18] This should be balanced with the fact that despite this, most men did not have much fighting experience, especially Lowlanders, and they did not generally go about armed, nor did most men who were not gentlemen own considerable numbers of weapons despite the popular image of the Highlander dashing about the glens armed to the teeth which existed at the time too: 'the meanest man among them is not without a Gun, a broad-sword, a Durk and target'.[19] Martin Martin says that 'since the invention of guns, they are very accustomed to use them, and carry their pieces with them wherever they go. They likewise learn to handle the broad sword and target'.[20]

A list of manpower in Blair Atholl and Glen Tilt from 1702 shows that fewer than 50 percent were armed in some way, while only 20 percent were equipped with both a sword and musket.[21] However, it is difficult

---

13 Pittock, *The Myth of the Jacobite Clans*, pp.50, 51, 59; D. Szechi. *The Jacobites: Britain and Europe, 1688–1788*, 2nd Edition (Manchester: Manchester University Press, 2019), p.116.

14 Szechi, *The Jacobites: Britain and Europe, 1688–1788*, p.115.

15 Skene 'n.' Dictionary of the Scots Language, 2004, Scottish Language Dictionaries Ltd, <https://www.dsl.ac.uk/entry/dost/skene> (accessed 16 Oct 2019).

16 Morer quoted in J. Oates, *The Battle of Killiecrankie, The first Jacobite Campaign 1689–1691* (Warwick: Helion & Company, 2018), p.51.

17 T. Kirke, *A Modern Account of Scotland; Being, An exact Description of the Country* (London, 1679), p.11.

18 Cheape and Grant, *Periods In Highland History*, p.150.

19 Anon., *An Historical Account of the Highlanders*, p.18.

20 M.A. Martin, *A Description of the Western Islands of Scotland, circa 1695* (Edinburgh: Birlinn, 1994). p.210.

21 A. Mackilliop, *More Fruitful than the Soil: Army, Empire and the Scottish Highlands 1715–1815* (East Linton: Tuckwell, 2000), p.7.

to be absolutely accurate about numbers of weapons that were held since the Disarming Act of 1716, which imposed fines for possessing arms and encouraged their surrender to the authorities; it was largely the loyal clans – that is, those loyal to the Government – that had complied, thus leaving the Jacobite clans potentially equipped for another attempt at a Rising.[22] While it is clear that certain areas of Scotland and certain clans were particularly pro-Jacobite, the Government in the early 1700s seemed to be quite complacent, despite the considerable and general distrust of the Scots and their loyalty to the new regime. Regardless of the fact that the failed Rising in 1708 had drawn attention to the support for the Jacobites in the north-east, the situation there and in the Highlands was essentially ignored by the Government, as was the general dislike of the Union by much of the population, certainly north of the Firth of Forth. Surprisingly therefore, there were very few Government agents in the North before the 1715 Rising, probably as few two in the whole of the Highlands.[23] This was despite the number of 'desperate men of dubious fortunes' who once recruited to the Jacobite cause were also the best source of possible government agents.[24] This contributed to a lack of information on both sides, since the Jacobites were working at a disadvantage as James and his court were in exile after the defeat in Ireland in 1692, and the Government had fewer people on the ground than might have been expected.

This book is concerned with the Jacobites in Scotland and throughout the time it discusses, the image of Scots and in particular the Highlanders which certainly outside Scotland, the two were often conflated, was that the Scots were wild and barbarian. Indeed, the Scots themselves, often portrayed Highlanders as such; in the 1500s Mary, Queen of Scots had 'wild Highland men' dressed in goatskins at her masques. Or the depiction of the wild Highlander on the seventeenth-century Speed map of Scotland, who was shown wearing nothing but animal skins. The King and Parliament regarded Highlanders as 'wild savages'. It was said that they were 'void of religioun' and therefore capable of 'maist detestabill, damnabill and odious murthers, fyiris, reveishing of wemen, witchcraft, and depredatiounis'.[25] The men of the Scots Army at Worcester in 1651 were described as barbarians.[26] William Cleland[27] in 1678 describes what he perceived as the Highlanders' disgusting personal habits, outlandish dress 'plaidin, with Hooding gray and worsted stuffs', and their habit of 'chaseing lasses'. Thomas Kirk[28] during his tour of Scotland in 1677, said that he would not travel further into the Highlands than Loch Ness. 'About the further end of this Lough are great fir-woods,

---

22 Mackilliop, *More Fruitful than the Soil*, p.2.
23 R. Clyde, *From Rebel to Hero: The Image of the Highlander 1745–1830* (East Linton: Tuckwell, 1998), p.2; Also Pittock, *The Myth of the Jacobite Clans*, p.54.
24 Szechi, *The Jacobites*, pp.32–33.
25 Mickel, '"Our Hielandmen": Scots in Court Entertainments at Home and Abroad 1507–1616', *Journal for the Society of Renaissance Studies* (2018), pp.1–19; Stroh, 'The Modern Nation-State and Its Others', pp.33–76.
26 Pittock, *The Myth of the Jacobite Clans*, p.16.
27 W. Donaldson, *The Jacobite Song: Political Myth and National Identity* (Aberdeen: Aberdeen University Press, 1988), p.50.
28 R. Thoresby, *Letters of Eminent Men, Addressed to Ralph Thoresby: First Published from the Originals*, vol. II (London: H. Colburn and R. Bentley, 1832), p.439.

but they are so full of rogues that we durst not see them: none dare pass the Highlands without a guard of ten or twelve, at the least.' Edmund Burt, in the 1720s, described Highlanders wearing their plaids like a cloak, but he also said that many people elsewhere in Britain believed that wearing a plaid allowed Highlanders to steal and thieve. In 1692 the Reverend Morer, an English clergyman, said that the Highlanders used their plaids to cover stolen goods. Thus, linking Highland dress with the idea of the supposed wildness and disregard for the rule of law of the Highlander and the Highlands.[29] Additionally, arguably eighteenth-century Whig propaganda equated the sense of cultural distance that they associated with the Highlands with political otherness in their perceived support for the Stuarts.[30] Certainly, post the '45, writers were keen to suggest ways in which the Highlands could be civilised and therefore remove the 'spirit of Jacobitism that already too much prevails. Enervate the good Endeavours of the King and Government for Establishing Order, and good harmony amongst the People.'[31]

It was during the seventeenth century that the idea of tartan and Highland dress – a short slashed doublet, in the seventeenth and then a short hip length coat (*còt*) in the eighteenth century with a belted plaid (*féileadh-mór*) worn over it with or without trews (*triubhas*) and the knitted blue bonnet – began to be associated with Stuart cause. As early as 1689, a Lowland lawyer such as 'Mr Drummond, the advocate' in Dundee's army was wearing the 'Highland habit': 'I was extremely surprised when I saw Mr Drunimond, the advocate, in Highland habit.'[32] In James Philip of Almerieclose's *The Grameid* of 1691, a long and rather baroque Latin poem about the 1689 Rising, tartan clothing is a symbol of the Jacobite army's struggle to restore Scotland. The poet, Iain Lom, the Bard of Keppoch criticised Lord MacDonell's frequent absences in the south and changed clothing, he suggested that his chieftain wear the Highland clothes again – and along with them return to Highland ways of life. '*Gur fada leam an Sasann thu, /'S a bhith 'gad chreach le spòrs/ B'fheàrr leam còt' is breacan ort/ Na pasbhin chur air cleò; Is tu bhith falbh gu h-aigeannach/ An triubhas chadaidh clò.* (You seem to me to be a long time in England, being ruined by gaming / I would prefer you in a coat and plaid / Than in the cloak which fastens / And that you should walk in a sprightly manner in trews made of tartan cloth.)[33] Burt described witnessing the women of a clan take great offence at one of their local gentry being dressed in Lowland style: 'I asked him wherein he had offended them? Upon this Question he laughed, and told me his great coat was the cause of their wrath;

---

29 For a discussion of this, see also Pittock, *The Myth of the Jacobite Clans*; Mickel, '"Our Hielandmen" : Scots in Court Entertainments at Home and Abroad 1507–1616', pp.1–19; P. Hume-Brown (ed.), *Early Travellers in Scotland* (Edinburgh: D. Douglas, 1891), p.29; S. Tuckett, 'Weaving the Nation: Scottish Clothing and Textile Cultures in the Long Eighteenth Century' (2010), unpublished PhD thesis.

30 Stroh, 'The Modern Nation-State and Its Others'.

31 Clyde, *From Rebel to Hero*, p.12.

32 G. Smythe, *Letters of John Grahame of Claverhouse, Viscount of Dundee, with Illustrative Documents* (Edinburgh: J. Bannatyne, 1826), p.47.

33 A. MacKenzie (ed.), *Orain Iain Luim, Songs of John, Bard of Keppoch* (Edinburgh: Published by the Scottish Academic Press for the Scottish Gaelic Texts Society, 1973), pp.125–6.

and that their reproach was, that he could not be contented with the garb of his ancestors, but had degenerated into a Lowlander, and condescended to follow their unmanly Fashions.'[34]

However, despite these complaints Lowland clothing was considered to be a mark of social standing since many of the Highland gentry and merchants wore it at least some of the time.[35] Burt says 'the gentlemen, magistrates, merchants, and shopkeepers, are dressed after the English manner, and make a good appearance, according to their several ranks'.[36] As does Martin Martin who states that 'persons of distinction of distinction wear the Garb in fashion in the South of England'.[37]

By the 1715 Rising, many of the men in the Jacobite Army, regardless of their place of origin, were dressed in Highland clothing and many others wore the plaid. Highland garb by this time might be considered to being on its way to becoming a sort of uniform for the Jacobites and after 1707, for those opposed to the Union of the Parliaments of Scotland and England, something that certainly happened with the army of Charles Edward Stuart during the last Jacobite Rising in 1745.

Laurence Oliphant of Gask ordered 'four blankets or Hyland plaids' to take with him in 1715'.[38] The Highland plaid was mostly but not exclusively made from brightly coloured tartan. There was also a similar plaid worn by many in the Lowlands, generally of a small black and white check or a plain fabric, quite often grey.[39] In 1689 Thomas Morer described the use of plaid by Lowlanders: 'Their habit is mostly English, saving that the meaner sort of men wear bonnets instead of hats, and pladds instead of cloaks.'[40]

Sir Walter Scott described it as:

> Maud or low country plaid. It is long piece of cloth about a yard wide over the left shoulder where it hangs loose something like a Spanish cloak wrap'd loosely round the waist like a scarf and from thence brought across the breast and the end thrown, It is not of Tartan but the natural colour of the wool with a very small black check which gives it greyish look'd.[41]

It was the way in which it was worn that changed according to the gender and geographical location.[42] William Sacheverell, Governor of the Isle of Man, wrote in 1688 about Highlanders: 'The usual outward habit of both sexes is

34 E. Burt, *Burt's Letters*, p.235.
35 S. Nenadic, *Lairds and Luxury: The Highland Gentry in Eighteenth-Century Scotland* (Edinburgh: John Donald, 2007), p.140.
36 Burt, *Burt's Letters*, p.48.
37 Martin, *A Description*, p.207.
38 T.L. Kington-Oliphant, *The Jacobite Lairds of Gask* (London: Published for the Grampian Club by C. Griffin & Co., 1870), p.28.
39 Tuckett, 'Weaving the Nation', p.50.
40 J.T. Dunbar, *History of Highland Dress* (London: Batsford, 1962), p.97.
41 W. Partington (ed.), *The Private Letter Book of Sir Walter Scott* (London: Hodder & Stoughton, 1930), p.379.
42 S. Nenadic, 'Necessities: Food and Clothing in the Long Eighteenth Century', in E. Foyster and C.A. Whatley (eds.), *A History of Everyday Life in Scotland, 1600–1800* (Edinburgh: Edinburgh University Press, 2010), pp.137–163.

the pladd. The women's much finer, the colours more lively, and the squares larger than the men's … The men wear theirs after another manner, especially when designed for ornament: it is loose and flowing, like the mantles our painters give their heroes.'[43]

It is likely that James VIII and III wore tartan in Scotland during the 1715 Rising, however no contemporary depictions exist. It is also in the period that this book covers that the Scots began to move from being from being stereotyped in English popular culture as blue bonnet wearers to being tartan wearers.[44] Indeed, as far back as 1603 when James VI took the throne in England, 'right Scotch plaids' were being sold in England and are evidence that tartan was already seen in England as 'symbolic of Scotland and Scottishness and not just the wild Highlander'.[45] There are numerous references in contemporary songs and political satire about the Highlanders' apparently insatiable sexual appetite.[46] In the *Night Walker*, published by Whig author John Dunton in 1696. he declares that 'all the whores in town are Jacobite' and describes how all the Jacobites 'leave a Campagne Wigg, an old Scarlet Coat, or Silverhilted Sword, and sometimes a Prince of Wale's Picture, or that of the late King and Queen in Pawn till they get Money'.[47]

> She would not have a Low-land laird / He wears the high heel'd shoes / She will marry Duncan Grahame / For Duncan wears his trews / she would have the highland man to row her in his plaidie.[48]

Tartans or rather their patterns or setts were not at this time specific to any particular clan although it does appear that some setts were more popular in particular areas. That said the MacDonalds might possibly have fought at Killiecrankie as a regiment wearing a plaid with similar colours, while in 1704, the Laird of Grant called out on 48 hours' notice the 'fencible men' of Badenoch and Strathspey for the Laird's 'hosting or hunteing'; each man was to be dressed in 'Heighland coates, trewes, and short hoes of Tartane of red and greine sett broad springed and also with gun, sword, pistoll and durk'.[49] Tartan was a cloth mostly made from a long wool worsted yarn generally in a 2/2 twill. A 2/2 twill has two warp threads, these were the two threads

---

43   D. Stewart, *Old and Rare Scottish Tartans* (Edinburgh, 1893), p.24.

44   G. Pentland, '"We Speak for the Ready": Images of Scots in Political Prints, 1707–1832', *The Scottish Historical Review*, vol. 90, No. 229, Part 1 (April 2011), pp.64–95.

45   M. Pittock, *Material Culture and Sedition, 1688–1760: Treacherous Objects, Secret Places* (Basingstoke: Palgrave Macmillan, 2013), p.84.

46   While the trope of the outsider coming to steal your women is obviously an old one, in this case it may at least in part be attributed to the differences in clothing that were perceived to make Highlanders (and therefore Jacobites) less moral, and more able to carry out illicit sexual liaisons without the restrictions of Lowland breeches.

47   J. Dunton, *The Night-walker: Or, Evening Rambles in Search after Lewd Women, with the Conferences Held with Them, &c.* (London, 1696).

48   W. Donaldson, *The Jacobite Song*, p.57. The song is called *Lizie Balie* and in it Lizie abandons her former soldier lover for the Highlander Duncan Grahame, at least in part because of his trews and plaid, giving up a life of relative ease in the Lowlands to wear 'Gowns of Tartain' in the north.

49   Stewart, *Old and Rare Scottish Tartans*, pp.27–28.

stretched longwise on a loom, crossing the two threads which were woven horizontally through the warp, this forms the pattern. The tartan was often bright almost gaudy. Looking at contemporary paintings and descriptions, it is possible to tell that the tartans were worn at this period mixed up, with the coat being one pattern and the plaid another, the trews another and so on to suit the taste and budget of the wearer. Although the plaid had been worn by many Scots for since at least the sixteenth century and of course Highland clothes were worn by Highlanders. It must be said that Highland clothes were certainly adopted by many as a political statement post the Union in 1707 and during the 1715 Rising.

2

Clavers and his Highland Men

Clavers and his highland men
Came down upo' the Ra' Man
Who being stout gave mony a Clout
The lads began to clou' them
With sword and Targe into their hand[1]

Major General The Viscount Dundee to July 1689,
Colonel Cannon,
General Thomas Buchan of Auchmacoy

Foot
Antrim's foot (picquets)
Cameron of Locheil
Farquharson of Inverey coy
MacDonald of Clanranald's
MacDonell of Glengarry
MacDonalds of Keppoch
MacDonalds of Sleat
Sir Alexander MacLean
Cormac O'Neil
Brigadier General Ramsay's Foot
Robertson of Struan
Stewarts of Appin
Frasers
Badenoch's men

Horse
Dundee's horse
Some 250 additional horse[2]

---

1   W. Donaldson, *The Jacobite Song*, p.25.
2   Oates, *The Battle of Killiecrankie*, p.90; Pittock, *The Myth of the Jacobite Clans*, p.186.

The men who fought in the first of the Jacobite Risings looked more like the popular idea of the Jacobites than majority of the men who fought in the subsequent Risings. Most of the army that fought under Claverhouse, Cannon, and Buchan were Highland men and so for the most part were wearing Highland clothes. Some of them even had beards and long hair and many of them fought with swords, dirks, targes and Lochaber axes.

The end of the seventeenth century was a period of very cold weather in Northern Europe and therefore much of the clothing worn by both elite and non-elite men was wool. In the context of Highland clothing this was a linen, sometimes a wool shirt, plaid, a coat, a waistcoat and short hose and trews (*truibhas*).

The Latin poem, *The Grameid* written by James Philip, tells us that for example 'the brave Glengarry leads three hundred illustrious youths, each of whom a tartan garb covers and 'a garment clothes their broad chest and flanks'.[3] Following Glengarry 'closely his brother Allan [historically this should be Angus] the brave with a hundred men all clothed in garments interwoven with the red stripe'.[4] This matches the descriptions of contemporary tartans which often did have red in them. Red was a particularly important colour in Gaelic culture. A lament for John MacLeod of Raasay, drowned in 1671, included the lines: 'S gur maith thigeadh dhuit breacan Air a lasadh Ie carnaid; 'S cha bu mhiosa dhuit triubhais A-'dol a siubhal nan sraidean'. ('And the tartan becomes you well; Shining with scarlet; And no worse for you indeed were trews; Going to travel the streets.') Cheape says that *gheibhte breacan* (scarlet tartan) was a stock phrase since the idea of red tartan was a commonplace idea.[5]

It has often been assumed that only home-grown, locally produced dyes were used in Highland dress and that these led to the colours of the clothing being muted and therefore authentic Highland clothing from this time must be muddy in colour, much like historic clothing from TV and film where peasants in particular are often portrayed dressed in clothes that are shades of mud. This idea is also fuelled by the fact that many of the extant pieces of clothing from this era are from bog bodies or have been otherwise damaged in some way, so the colours are naturally faded or spoiled. However, the actual evidence must lead to other conclusions. Dyes like cochineal and indigo began to be available throughout Europe just around the period of the first Rising and certainly by 1715; Highlanders had access to them as of course did other Scots. The Import Book of Dumfries records a Scots ship returning from the Netherlands in 1688/9 carrying woad (a dye which gives blue), galls (used to make black ink or dye), madder (red, and in fact the British army used madder for their coats), alum, copperas (these two are mordants which were used to fix the dye) and brazilwood (a highly

---

3   A.D. Murdoch and J. Philip, *The Grameid: An Heroic Poem Descriptive of the Campaign of Viscount Dundee in 1689, and Other Pieces* (Edinburgh: Printed at the University Press by T. and A. Constable for the Scottish History Society, 1888), p.123.

4   It is this reference that implies that the MacDonalds might have worn a matching plaid.

5   H. Cheape, 'Gheibhtebreacaincharnaid ("Scarlet Tartans Would be Got …"): the Re-invention of Tradition'; in I. Brown (ed.), *From Tartan to Tartanry: Scottish Culture, History and Myth* (Edinburgh: Edinburgh University Press, 2012), pp.13–31.

Lord Mungo Murray (*Am Morair Mungo Moireach*) by John Michael Wright.
In this portrait, painted just before Killiecrankie, the youthful Lord Mungo is dressed for hunting in his plaid, he carries a flintlock and a pair of the typically Scottish ramshorn pistols in his belt with gold pickers, used for cleaning out the pistol's touch hole. The very full sleeves of his shirt can be seen through his fashionable slashed short doublet. He also has a dirk with a simply decorated hilt and another smaller knife in the sheath, a powder horn and three brass measures, each of which contains a charge of powder. His sword is one of the very early types of Highland guard; his short hose are gartered with a silk ribbon and his shoes with decorated tongues and small buckles are similar to those worn by Lord Duffus. His servant has a plaid and trews. He is carrying a bow as was used for hunting and may have been carried by some of those fighting at Killiecrankie. (Image © National Galleries of Scotland)

prized red dye from Brazil).[6] At this time, the New Mills Cloth Manufactory in Haddington, near Edinburgh was importing dyes including madder, logwood (which will give a blue or purple) and woad; sumac – native to southern Europe and often used to dye leather, galls as well as a variety of mordants.[7] In 1684, imported goods such as indigo, cochineal, tobacco and spices were to be found in Highland tacksmen's houses and the accounts of a merchant in Campbelltown in 1672 show that he had indigo and cochineal as well as tobacco, sugar and wine for sale.[8] The dye stuff indigo had probably reached even the very remote areas such as St Kilda by 1700.[9] Additionally, Martin writing in the 1690s discussed ships which called in at the Western Highlands so even those living in isolated areas were aware of the outside world and what was available.[10] Peddlers and others travelled from place to place carrying small items like buttons, ribbons, lace, dyes and tobacco.[11]

Plaids with a brown or yellow ground seem to have been more common for as everyday wear for ordinary clansmen. Philip described the men of the Hebrides as being dressed in 'yellow and blue'. The wealthier you were, the brighter your clothes were in Highland culture, so the front ranks of the Dundee's army consisting as it did of the clan gentlemen would have been very colourful. MacNeill of Barra[12] had 'so many colours woven into his plaid as the rainbow in the clouds shows in the sunlight'. There is no evidence of a clan tartan at this time in the sense of one tartan with a specific pattern being the preserve of one clan.

The plaid itself (*féileadh-mór or breacain an fhéilidh*, literally great wrap or tartan wrap), was a rectangle of cloth, usually of wool, frequently with a tartan pattern but not always: 'Many of 'em have nothing under these Garments besides Wastcoats and Shirts, which descent no lower than the Knees, and they so gird 'em about the Middle as to give 'em the same length as the Linen under 'em, and thereby supply the defect of Drawers and Breeches.'[13]

The plaid was a multi-use garment,[14] capable of being a warm garment during the day and a bed at night. Burt noted that when Highlanders had to

---

6   J. Burnett, K. Mercer and A. Quye, 'The Practice of Dyeing Wool in Scotland *c*. 1790–*c*.1840', *Folk Life*, 42:1 (2003), pp.7–31.
7   W.R. Scott (ed.), *The Records of a Scottish Cloth Manufactory at New Mills, Haddingtonshire, 1681–1703* (Edinburgh: Scottish History Society, 1905), p.13; Burnett, Mercer and Quye, 'The Practice of Dyeing Wool in Scotland'.
8   Cheape and Grant, *Periods in Highland History*, p.162.
9   Burnett, Mercer and Quye, 'The Practice of Dyeing Wool in Scotland'; H. Cheape, 'Gheibhte breacain charnaid ('Scarlet Tartans Would be Got …'): the Re-invention of Tradition', in I. Brown (ed.), *From Tartan to Tartanry: Scottish Culture, History and Myth* (Edinburgh: Edinburgh University Press, 2012).
10   Martin, *A Description*, p.357.
11   J. Burnett, K. Mercer and A. Quye, 'The Practice of Dyeing Wool in Scotland *c*. 1790–*c*. 1840', *Folk Life*, 42:1 (2003), pp.7–31.
12   Murdoch and Philip, *The Grameid*, p.128.
13   *Collectanea de Rebus Albanicis, Consisting of Original Papers and Documents Relating to the History of the Highlands and Islands of Scotland*, ed. by the Iona Club (Edinburgh: T.G. Stevenson, 1847), p.43.
14   T.G. Stevenson (ed.), *Collectanea de Rebus Albanicis, Consisting of Original Papers and Documents Relating to the History of the Highlands and Islands of Scotland* (Edinburgh: The Iona Club, 1847), p.43. 'That they not only serve them for Cloaths by Day in case of necessity but were Pallats or Beds in the Night at such times as they travelled and had not opportunities for better Accommodation, and for that reason in Campaigns were not unuseful'.

spend a night out on the hills, they would soak the plaid in a river and would wrap themselves up in the wet cloth. This combination of 'wet fabric and warm body then made a steam like that of a boiling kettle' and apparently kept the wearer warm.[15] It should also be noted that there were specific bed plaids which appear quite frequently on inventories, there were several in the inventory of the House of the Binns from 1688 for example.[16] The length of the plaid seems to have been about five yard (4.5m) lengths, Martin Martin says seven double ells (6.75m) although plaids as long as nine yards (8.2m) were mentioned and one poet says 10 yards, however it is likely that these are the lengths before a plaid was sewn up. The plaid would be folded lengthwise into rough pleats, not the lovely flat front apron neat pleats of a modern kilt, the pleats went all the way round, there was no apron as on a modern kilt. There is some evidence that some of the plaids of the later eighteenth-century Highland revival had internal drawstrings. It is unlikely that any of the plaids at this time did so since it would have reduced their versatility and it is not mentioned in any contemporary account. Therefore, it seems more likely that the plaids of the time were simply pulled together using a belt. As Iain Lom says in his poem *A song to the Army of King James*:

> *Bu fhliuch a' mhadainn a thog sinn ar breacain/ 'S a chaidh sinn air astar gus an tiagh 'gan robh chairt/'N uair rinn eirigh gun d'rinn sinn ar eideadh Is chaidh sinn 'nar leum fo na cnapanna-saic*

> (Wet was the morning, we picked up our plaids. And set out on the journey to the house where our plan lay / When we arose, we belted our plaids and hastily shouldered our knapsacks)[17]

Martin describes it as 'pleated from the Belt to the Knee very nicely'.[18] Once this was done whether with help or alone, then the other half of the plaid was as Martin said 'tied on the breast with a bodkin of bone or wood' or sometimes a pin of a finer metal, the choice of which was dependant like all these things on status. The plaid was not fastened using a brooch as it is sometimes now, and it was quite frequently during the nineteenth century.

The gap between the belted plaid and hose was quite large as the plaid was worn short, unlike the modern kilt. Edmund Burt, who clearly disapproved of the amount of leg on display, wrote that, 'The common habit of the ordinary highlander is far from being acceptable to the eye a small part of the plaid, which is not so large as the former, is set in folds and girt round the waist to make of it a small petticoat that reaches halfe way down the thigh.'[19]

---

15 Burt, *Burt's Letters*, pp.197–8.

16 J. Dalyell and J. Beveridge (ed.), 'Inventory of the Plenishing of the House of the Binns at the Date of the Death of General Thomas Dalyell, 21st August 1683. Edited from the Original Documents in the Family Records', *Proceedings of the Society of Antiquaries of Scotland*, 58 (1924), pp.344–370.

17 Mackenzie, *Orain Iain Luim, Songs of John, Bard of Keppoch: Oran Air Feachd Righ Semas*, pp.184–5.

18 Martin, *A Description*, p.208.

19 Burt, *Burt's Letter*, p.232.

'Their calves bound with red buskin'[20] as Philip described the men. Many contemporary accounts say that the bias-cut cloth hose (*osan*) worn with Highland dress were kept up by scarlet garters: *Luchd nan osanan ballach, 's nan gartanan gle-dhearg* (Men of the tartan hose, and the bright red garters).[21] Philip also described Sir Ewen Cameron of Lochiel as having 'his tartan hose gartered around his calf'.[22] Thomas Kirk who visited Scotland about 10 years before the Rising described the men he saw as having: 'their stockings, rolled up about the calves of their legs and tied with their garter, their knee and thigh being naked'.[23] Sacheverell, wrote in 1688: 'Their thighs are bare, with brawny muscles. Nature has drawn all her streaks bold and masterly; what is covered is only adapted to necessity – a thin brogue on the foot, a short buskin of various colours on the legg, tied above the calf with a striped pair of garters'.[24] *Mar ghealbhradain di chosan / Le d' ghearr- osan mu d' chalpa* (Like bright salmon your legs / With short hose round your calves).[25] Morer made it clear that the hose were sewn, not knitted. 'Those who have Stockings make 'em generally of the same piece with their Pladds, not knit or weaved, but sow'd together, and they tie 'em below the Knee with Tufted Garters.'[26] In 1678, writing about the Highland Host in Ayr, a letter in the Wodrow MS says that 'the fashion of their wild apparel, not one of ten of them hath breeches, yet hose and shoes are their greatest need'.[27] Interestingly, the laird of Grant's specifications for his men 'Heighland coates, trewes, and short hoes of Tartane' implies that they, at least, were wearing short hose with their trews. Since covered legs and the wearing of stockings was seen as a mark of respectability and money elsewhere in Britain, it was confusing to contemporaries that not only did poor Scots men expose their legs but so did those who had money.

There are references to clansmen casting their plaids off before fighting during the campaign and when they did so they would tuck or knot their long shirts between their legs. Philip said that when they fought, 'they cast their brogues of bull's hide and make a pile of their plaids and thus striped prepared for battle'.[28] However not everyone did this at Killiecrankie since when John Macrae of Inversheil was shot in the thigh – 'the ball having carried the wound the clothe of this belted plade and the trewes that he wore under them, the woolen sid so wrankle the fleshe that with his hard travail'.[29] He obviously had not thrown off his plaid before being wounded. One account from a Jacobite officer says that they 'threw away' plads. haversacks and all other utinsils[30] and marched resolutely and deliberately to fight in their shirts and doublets'. This tells us a few things: firstly, that the men were wearing

20 Murdoch and Philip, *The Grameid*, p.123.
21 Dunbar, *History of Highland Dress*, p.42.
22 Murdoch and Philip, *The Grameid*, p.132.
23 Dunbar, *Highland Dress*, p.42.
24 *Stewart, Old and Rare Scottish Tartans*, p.24.
25 *Mo Run Geal Og* – Christina Ferguson.
26 T. Morer, *A Short Account of Scotland. Being a Description of the Nature of that Kingdom, and what the Constitution of it is in Church and State* (1702). ECCO, accessed 17 March 2019; pp.8–9.
27 Quoted in Stewart, *Old and Rare Scottish Tartans*, pp.19–20.
28 Quoted in Oates, *The Battle of Killiecrankie*, p.102.
29 Stewart, *Old and Rare Scottish Tartans*, p.23.
30 Murdoch and Philip, *The Grameid*, p.184.

doublets – not just shirts, additionally that they were carrying haversacks or pocks – just Lord George Murray ordered for his men in 1745 so that they could carry their rations and interestingly 'other utinsils' – possibly canteens.[31] Iain Lom mentioned haversacks in his poem. *A Song To the Army of King James*: *Bu fhliuch a' mhadainn a thog sinn ar breacain/ 'S a chaidh sinn air astar gus an tiagh 'gan robh chairt/'N uair rinn eirigh gun d'rinn sinn ar eideadh Is chaidh sinn 'nar leum fo na cnapanna-saic* (When we arose we belted our plaids and hastily shouldered our knapsacks[32]).[33] Unfortunately, no one gives any more details on these. It is probable though they were similar to the two extant examples in the Netherlands, a long tube like bag made of leather tied, possibly a draw string closure at each end for carrying food.

The tartan that they wore was in a variety of different setts and they frequently had on several different patterns at any one time with their hose being of one pattern, their plaid or trews another and their coat still another as can be seen in contemporary portraiture. Looking at the development of the setts it seems most likely that patterns were simply passed on from weaver to weaver, possibly travelling like gossip and other goods along the well-worn trade routes through the glens and over the hills so different districts would end up with similar patterns. The width of the cloth, produced generally by professional male weavers like all cloth until the industrial revolution, was dictated by the looms available and so was commonly between 26 and 30 inches. Therefore in order to make the belted plaid, two widths would be sewn up.[34] Lord James Murray, in his very comprehensive inventory in 1715 had '2 highland plaids not made and 1 made'.[35] In general, plaids were made from worsted fabric, that is a cloth that had been combed rather than carded so all the fibres ran in the same direction. The finished plaiding was sold in a special ell that was 38.4 inches; thus approximately 1.4 inches longer than the standard Scottish ell to allow for shrinkage.

With the plaid or trews, elite men wore short doublets decorated with lace, the sleeves wide, short and slashed – some seem to have been tartan and others a single colour quite frequently red. 'Their doublet, breeches and stockings of a stuff they called plaid striped across red and yellow with short cloakes of the same.' Plebeian men wore similar short doublets, although theirs were generally duller in colour and with no decoration. Lochiel's doublet is described as 'tricoloured' which sounds very much like tartan and

---

31 Quoted in J.M. Hill, *Celtic Warfare 1595–1793* (unknown place and publisher; 1986), p.72.

32 Knapseck 'n.' *Dictionary of the Scots Language*, 2004, Scottish Language Dictionaries Ltd, <https://www.dsl.ac.uk/entry/dost/knapseck> (accessed 18 November 2019) quoted in this entry 'the town should furnish each soldier with a knapseck carieing provisions Aberdeen 1647' accessed December 2019

33 Mackenzie, *Orain Iain Luim, Songs of John, Bard of Keppoch: Oran Air Feachd Righ Semas*, pp.184–5.

34 Weavers of wool, like tailors were almost all male. There is some evidence that women might weave linen at home but this practice was less common by the end of the seventeenth century except for those who were earning a living by doing so. Spinning, done mostly with a distaff, was almost without exception done by women. Not all plaids were woven in the Highlands. Many were woven in Stirling and Glasgow, and later in the eighteenth century the best plaids were produced in Stirling.

35 Stewart-Murray and Anderson, *Chronicles of the Atholl and Tullibardine Families*, p.cviii.

'trimmed all around with gold lace' by Philip.[36] Coll MacDonald is described by him as 'kapochus aureus' – golden coated which definitely gives the impression that his coat at least had plenty of gold lace. Many appear to have been wearing coats of one colour, not tartans. James Malcolm stated that 'he sawe a young gentleman, whom they called young Sir Donald Macdonald of Slait, command a regiment at the feight of Kilichrankie, and that he saw him command the same regiment at Keppoch, and that he wore a red coat.'[37] James Malcolm again said 'that he sawe a man called the Laird of Auchterrawe, who came from Ireland to my Lord Dundie at Lochaber, and who wes sent back to Ireland, and that he wes a grosse man, and hade a blewe coat, and that he was in arms'.[38]

Trews were long, tight hose cut on the bias to allow for stretch and movement. They were often worn in the winter, longer journeys or for riding. *Triubhas teann feadh bheann is blealach, Coiseachd bhonn get rom do mheallag.* (in tight fitting trews you traversed mountain and pass on foot, although heavy was your paunch).[39] Some men wore them with a plaid, as did John Macrae of Inversheil. Kirk says that they were 'all on a piece and straight to them, plaid colour'. Martin described them as: 'Many of the people wear trowis, some of them are very fine woven, like stockings, made of cloath; some are coloured, and others striped; the latter are as well shap'd as the former, lying close to the body from the middle downwards, and tied round with a belt above the haunches'.[40]

'There is a square piece of cloth which hangs down before' is clearly illustrated in a picture after de Witt called Lowland Wedding or Village Dance in the National Museum of Scotland. As Martin said, trews were generally made from tartan and like many other items of male clothing at this time would have been made by a tailor, the exceptions normally being shirts and if worn, underwear. Like peddlers, a small number of tailors travelled throughout the Highlands in the summer. Elite men could of course send to larger towns or cities for tailors or cloth. Elite Highland men at this time did not wear the Highland habit all the time, however it is likely that most would have taken both Lowland and Highland clothes on campaign. Martin tells us that 'Persons of distinction wear the Garb in Fashion in the South of Scotland'.[41] The accounts of the Macleods of Dunvegan show that they were having clothes made elsewhere by a tailor, importing fashionable hats, gold buttons and sending away for worsted stockings.[42]

Those men who were wearing underwear are likely to have been wearing two types. Firstly short drawers like those on Charles II's effigy in Westminster Abbey. These were made of silk, although it is reasonable to assume that most

---

36 Murdoch and Philip, *The Grameid*, p.132.
37 Smythe, *Letters of John Grahame of Claverhouse*, p.41.
38 Smythe, *Letters of John Grahame of Claverhouse*, p.64.
39 Iain Lom, *An Ciaran Mabach* (the stammering Ciaran).
40 Martin, *A Description*, p.206.
41 Martin, *A Description*, p.207.
42 R.C. Macleod, *The Book of Dunvegan. Being Documents from the Muniment Room of the MacLeods of MacLeod at Dunvegan Castle, Isle of Skye* (Aberdeen: Printed for the Third Spalding Club, 1938), pp.206–7.

would have been made from linen, fastened with ribbons at the front and in fact they looked not dissimilar to modern boxer shorts. The second type of drawers were long with stirrups: 'a pair of longe linnen drawes to put under breeches', costing seven shillings, were bought for the Duke of Albemarle's effigy in 1670.[43]

Dundee continued to wear his scarlet coat during the campaign; with gold lace. At James's coronation three years before, it had been noted that the officers wore scarlet whereas the soldiers wore red.[44] His coat would have been lined and faced in red. The idea of facing in the regimental colours for officers was only just being developed but it is unlikely that Dundee's coat faced or lined in yellow as those of his men were. His hat would have been made of imported beaver with white feathers, officers also wore crimson scarves or sashes, fringed with gold.[45] Buchan and Cannon as King's officers would also have continued to wear clothing very similar to that of Dundee. In November 1688, Dundee had bought 'ride cloth' from the New Cloth Mills in Haddington.[46] At Killiecrankie, he had apparently changed his coat to a one that was described as being 'silver and buff'. He may have worn a green sash.[47] Green had long been a significant colour for the Stuarts, although prior to 1688 it had Whig associations in particular with the Green Ribbon Club.[48] Coloured ribbons had long been way of telling which party or faction a man adhered to – red and blue ribbons for James as Duke of York and Monmouth respectively were used a few years before during the Exclusion Crisis. This was in direct contrast to the next century when blue began to be used as a Tory colour, as can been seen in many eighteenth-century portraits of English Jacobites in particular.[49]

The Royal Regiment of Scots Horse, which Dundee had been commander of until King James VII and II had left for France, had gone south in 1688 when William had landed and on their return from England Dundee's troop had remained loyal to the Stuarts. They wore red coats with brass buttons, lined and faced in yellow unlike the English Royal regiments whose coats were faced in blue.[50] It is possible that like MacDonald of Glencoe they wore a buffcoat, however the information on that is not clear since there is a suggestion that they stopped wearing them in 1686. They had uncocked black hats with a yellow hat band which is likely to have been edged in yellow tape. Brown

---

43 P. Cunnington and C. Willet, *The History of Underclothes* (London: Michael Joseph, 1951), p.60.

44 Brian Lyndon, 'Military Dress and Uniformity 1680–1720', *Journal of the Society for Army Historical Research*, vol. 54, no. 218 (1976), pp.108–120.

45 S. Ede-Borrett, *The Army of James II 1685–1688: The Birth of the British Army* (Solihull: Helion & Co., 2017), pp.48, 132.

46 Scott, *The Records of a Scottish Cloth Manufactory at New Mills*, p.201.

47 C.A. Fforde, *A Summer in Lochaber: The Jacobite Rising of 1689* (Isle of Colonsay: House of Lochar, 2002), p.149.

48 Founded in the 1670s, it was an exclusionist club, that is the exclusion of Catholics from the succession. See Pittock, *Material Culture and Sedition*, p.96. The Whigs themselves did not want a Catholic monarch and saw themselves as the enemies of absolutism and therefore were resolutely anti-Jacobite.

49 Pittock, *Material Culture and Sedition*, p.81; E. Legon, 'Bound up with Meaning: The Politics and Memory of Ribbon Wearing in Restoration England and Scotland', *Journal of British Studies*, 56 (2017), pp 27–50.

50 Ede-Borrett, *The Army of James II*, p.132; C. Dalton, *The Scots Army 1661–88* (London: Eyre & Spottiswoode, 1909), p.81.

leather gauntlets were issued to them. They wore over-knee riding boots and buff coloured breeches.[51] A few years before this Dundee had petitioned the Privy Council to be allowed import from England 150 ells of red cloth, 40 ells of white cloth, and 550 dozen of buttons presumably to clothe his men.[52]

The Irishmen from Antrim had been raised by Nicholas Purcell, one of those Irish Catholic gentlemen who had taken advantage of James VII and II's relaxation of the restrictions on Catholics to join the Army, and then remained loyal to James; they were described as the 'yellow horse'. It is actually not clear from the few descriptions that exist that their uniforms were actually yellow, or whether at this time it was only the officers who were in yellow with the men in grey or undyed coats. The 300 dismounted dragoons were recruited from Purcell's tenants, kinsmen and other followers. Properly dragoons should have been wearing black over knee boots for horse and foot service however it seems unlikely that these hastily raised, and generally poorly equipped troops would all have had these when in Scotland. They were described as 'newly-raised, naked, undisciplined'.[53] They were essentially wearing their civilian clothes: plain wool breeches or possibly trews as found at Dungiven in Ireland, a linen shirt and perhaps knitted wool stockings under the coat which had been given to them by the Regiment.[54] *Cha robh am faicinn bòideach;/.../ Bu chosamhla an gleus ri treudan bhèistean/Na ri luchd cèile còire'* (the sight of them was not lovely / their get up was more like the herds of beasts than men of justice),[55] which suggests that they were definitely not very well dressed. MacAilean suggests that their bonnets were coloured under which they had tucked their hair and their shirts were tucked up under their armpits. He also mentions that they are shoeless, however it is not clear whether they had, like many of the Highlanders, cast their shoes off to fight or if they had no shoes at all. Contemporary reports suggest that they landed in Argyllshire with 300 troops and 60 horse having been transported there by three French men-of-war and several other vessels from Carrickfergus. Purcell had brought with him 35 barrels of powder, ball, match and flint.

With Highland dress the majority of men wore thin soled pumps fastened with laces. Martin Martin said, 'The generality now wear Shoes, having one thin Sole only, and shaped after the right and left Foot so that what is for one Foot, will not serve the other.'[56] The shoes worn by the Highlanders had no heels, hence the shaping for left and right, since seventeenth-century shoes with heels were made straight-lasted; the same wooden last was used for both feet. Naturally those who could afford it wore fashionable shoes with heels

---

51 Ede-Borrett, *The Army of James II*, p.132.
52 R. Chambers, *Domestic Annals of Scotland, from the Revolution to the Rebellion of 1745*, vol. II (Edinburgh: W. & R. Chambers, 1860), p.432.
53 Quoted in Fforde, *A Summer in Lochaber*, p.119.
54 Knitted stockings were associated with bog body finds at Tawnamore in Ireland, as were shoes, however the description of the men as naked lends itself to a suggestion of shirt and breeches/hose and not much else. See D. Wilcox, 'Scottish Late Seventeenth-Century Male Clothing (Part 2): The Barrock Estate Clothing Finds Described', *Costume*, vol. 51, Issue 1, March (2017), pp.28–53.
55 Iain MacAilein Quoted in Fforde, *A Summer in Lochaber*, p.120.
56 Martin, *A Description of the Western Islands of Scotland*, p.207.

or boots if riding; indeed, it still possible to see Sir Ewen Cameron's boots at the Clan Cameron Museum at Achnacarry and Sir John Foulis in 1679 spent £14 on a new pair of black boots and £14 10s on black 'shoes and galashoes'.[57] Lochiel himself is supposed to have fought barefooted at Killiecrankie. Bare-footedness was generally more frequent amongst Scots women than it was for men, and it must be assumed that the demands of being on campaign would tend to encourage most to wear shoes, although there are accounts of men fighting barefoot. 'They cast aside their brogues of bull's hide',[58] says *The Grameid*, and Mackay says 'they attack bare footed, without any cloathing but their shirts, and a little Highland dowblet'.[59] According to Martin, shoes were made from several different animal skins, such as deer, cow or horse, seal on Orkney, and intriguingly goose necks on St Kilda.[60] He describes their shoes as being 'a piece of the hide of a deer, cow or Horse with the hair on'. A description of a skirmish in 1685 during the Argyll rebellion has *ha sinn uile 'nar luaine/Dol a thualag air cais-bhe art/ Sinn 'nar luidh' a ir an l e acainn / 'S sinn ag feithe amh nrun marcach; Bha sinn ullamh gu teine, 's gu iomairt nan glas-lann -- Fios a thaineadh mu dheireadh Dol gu'r ceirinnin dachaidh!* (We were all in a bustle to cast off our footwear, as we lay on the hillside awaiting the horsemen. We were ready to fire, and to ply the grey swords, but the order that eventually came was to return to our quarters).[61]

Plebeian men in the Highlands wore their hair long and loose, elite men like their peers elsewhere often wore wigs. By 1694, there were 29 wigmakers in the centre of Edinburgh alone.[62] Most likely, while moving about the Highlands, they would be wearing a campaign wig. Sir John Foulis ordered himself one in 1695 for £24 Scots.[63] A campaign wig was a travelling wig with a twisted lock of hair on each side. Although Dundee unfashionably wore his own hair during the raid on Edinglassie, where he got ready for battle by 'pressing his long hair up under a gleaming helmet'.[64]

The blue knitted bonnet seems to have come into widespread use in the 1500s, and was worn throughout Scotland. 'They cover their heads with bonnets or thrum caps, not unlike those of our servitors, tho' of a better consistence to keep off the weather. They are blue, grey or sad colour as purchaser sees fit; and are sometimes lined according the according to the quality to the quality of their master'.[65] These bonnets were almost all

57 A.W.C. Hallen, *The Account Book of Sir John Foulis of Ravelston, 1671–1707* (Edinburgh: printed at the University Press by T. and A. Constable for the Scottish History Society, 1894), p.17.
58 Quoted in Oates, *The Battle of Killiecrankie*, p.102.
59 H. Mackay, J. Maitland Hog, P. Fraser Tyler and A. Urquhart, *Memoirs of the War Carried on in Scotland and Ireland, M.DC.LXXXIX.–M.DC.XCI: with an appendix of original papers* (Edinburgh: Maitland Club, 1833), p.51.
60 Martin, *A Description of the Western Islands of Scotland*, pp.207, 374, 455–456.
61 *Latha Chearm Loch-Fine* (The Day of the battle at the Head of Loch Fyne), by Alexander Robertson of Bohespic.
62 Wilcox, D, 'Scottish Late Seventeenth-Century Male Clothing: Some Context for the Barrock Estate Finds', *Costume*, vol. 50, no 2 (2016), pp.150–162.
63 Hallen, *The Account Book of Sir John Foulis of Ravelston*, p.185.
64 Quoted in Fforde, *A Summer in Lochaber*, p.149.
65 Morer, Quoted in Dunbar, *History of Highland Dress*, p.45.

knitted.[66] They were generally blue although slanted to one side some were russet, grey or green, they were worn flat on the head not slanted or like a modern cap. The Stewarts of Appin may have worn fur bonnets – 'brave Stewart of Appin prepares his arms and, with the whole body of clansmen, he leaves the shores bordering the Leven, rich in fish … Him, two hundred men follow to dread war, all of them tall, terrible in form and in arms, and wearing on their lofty heads fur bonnets'.[67]

'The Glencoe men were very remarkable, who had for their ensigne a faire bish of heath, displayed on the head of a staff'.[68] *The Grameid* says that they (Glengarry, Clan Ranald, Keppoch Sleat, Glencoe) carry 'into battle, as the emblem of their race, a bunch of wild heather hung from the point of a quivering spear'.[69] Other clans sometimes wore a clan badge in the form of a plant on their hats; bog myrtle for the Campbells, pine for the Grants or oak for Camerons.

Men in the late seventeenth-century Highlands often wore beards and moustaches. This was in contrast to the fashion elsewhere which was to be clean shaven as it would be in the next century. The men who fought in the first Jacobite Rising seem to have had particularly fine beards. Philip described Lochiel's beard and moustache as 'curled as the moon's horn' and Glencoe is described as 'rolling his wild eyes, the horns of his twisted beard curled backwards'.[70]

---

66 Virtually the only extant example of an exception to this is the hat from the Barrock estate finds, as it is cloth.
67 Murdoch and Philip, *The Grameid*, pp.143–4.
68 Cheape and Grant, *Periods In Highland History*, p.183.
69 Murdoch and Philip, *The Grameid*, p.128.
70 Murdoch and Philip, *The Grameid*, pp.124, 132.

3

After the gun, the sword ready

Luchd nam breacan, luchd nam breacan
A leigadh le mointich
A' foibh gu dian a' foibh dian
Gun stad re pris, an arbugh
An deudh a ghunna an claidheamh ullamh
(The men in plaid, the men in plaid
Who would rush down the hillside
Pressing on keenly, pressing on keenly
Stopping for nothing, in order
After the gun, the sword ready)

The men who joined Dundee after he raised the standard at Dudhope and then throughout the summer 'in Logh-whaber, skipping from one Hill to another, like wild-fire' used and carried a variety of weapons.[1] In 1679 the Macleans surrendered 185 swords, 95 guns, three pistols, five Lochaber axes and a two-handed sword.[2]

S b 'fhearr gu ' n tigeadh iad fhat hast /Clann Ghi lleathain nan tuagh/ 's cha bhiodh sgian arm am fraighe /No claidheamh an truaill/Bheirte mach na h-airm chatha/ 's cha bhiodh an latha sin buan/S ged bu ghuineach na Dui hnich, 's iad Siol Chuinn a bha cruaidh (I wish that Clan Maclean of the battle axes would still come, for not a knife would be left on the shelf, nor a sword in the scabbard. The fighting arms would be brought forth, and the battle would not last long, for though the Campbells are venomous, it is Clan Donald who are hardy).[3]

This is perhaps the only Jacobite campaign where there were more swords carried and used than guns. It was also fought almost entirely by Highlanders, which helped to cement the erroneous idea that all Jacobites were Highlanders, and all Highlanders, Jacobite. Swords were really

---

1   E.W.M. Balfour-Melville, *An Account of the Proceedings of the Estates in Scotland, 1689–1690* (Edinburgh: Scottish History Society, 1954), p.105.
2   Pittock, *The Myth of the Jacobite Clans*, p.169.
3   Iain Lom, quoted in 'The Sources, particularly the Celtic Sources, for the History of the Highlands in the Seventeenth Century' (1939), Unpublished PhD thesis, p.205.

A Scottish basket hilt from the end of the seventeenth century or beginning of the eighteenth, similar in style to many of those carried at both Killiecrankie and Sheriffmuir. It has an iron hilt. The initials AF are on the blade. It is unlikely that this blade was ever seen or touched by the semi-mythical Andrea Ferrera, so his initials were supposed to be a mark of quality. (Image © National Museums Scotland)

important in Gaelic culture; part of the heroic image of the chief and clan gentlemen, they appear in poetry frequently and as can be seen from surrenders like that above they were carried in considerable numbers by those of the gentry and tacksmen. Additionally, the large two-handed sword or claymore was more or less obsolete by this point – hence why there is 'ane two handed sword' which was probably used for ceremonial purposes rather than actual fighting. The other 185 swords and the majority of those carried at Killiecrankie, the Haughs of Cromdale or Dunkeld will have been basket-hilted swords (*claidheamh mor*) or back swords (*claidheamh cuil*) with one cutting edge. The blades of these swords like nearly all Scottish basket hilted swords were foreign, often German. There were some Scottish hangers made in Scotland, notably in Kilmaurs not far from Kilmarnock. There is only one Scottish hanger known to be still in existence. It was made by David Biggart of Kilmaurs with a fine tortoiseshell grip and silver inlay, and it is now in the collection of Glasgow Museums.[4] The majority of sword blades were imported into Scotland and then attached by a sword slipper or armourer, most of whom were actually based in the Lowlands. Scotland was never a particularly significant manufacturer of sword blades and they were easy to buy abroad. The armourer would make the hilt. Throughout the late seventeenth and eighteenth centuries these developed distinctive features, and by the mid 1700s it was possible to tell where in Scotland the hilt had been made – the best being made in Stirling. '*Ma ghaol an Tàinistear ùr/'S a gheur Spàineach 'na smùid/Cha b'e 'n t-ùmaidh air chùl sgéithe e* (Beloved by me is the young heir apparent with his sharp Spanish blade smoking in his hand; he was no poltroon behind a shield).[5] The Spanish blade here was not necessarily made in Spain but Toledo steel from Spain was reputed to be the best so the sword blade was supposed to be of the best quality; in the same way that blades often had Andrea Ferrara's signature on them after the Italian sixteenth-century swordsmith. Many of the sword blades would have been blued – Iain Lom mentions their 'dark blue blades'. Colonel Dalyell's inventory from 1685 had 12 swords: eight broadswords, three whingers (a sort of hanger) and a chable – a short curved sword. One of the whingers had three smaller 'knyves' in the sheath also.[6] A witness, John Osburn, described MacDonald of Keppoch as armed with 'a steel targe, a broadsword, and pistol'.[7] Iain Lom in a poem to the Marquess of Atholl talks of '*O 's iomadh fear goirseid/ Le ghunna boidheach 's lann dubhghorm/Le 'n cuinnseiribh caola 'S an taoimeun 'gan giulan* (Many a man with cuirass, fine gun and dark-blue blade, with their slender wingers supported by straps).[8] *The Grameid* tells us

---

4   T. Capwell, *The Real Fighting Stuff: Arms and Armour at Glasgow Museums* (Glasgow, Glasgow City Council (Museums), 2007), p.94.

5   MacKenzie, *Orain Iain Luim, Songs of John, Bard of Keppoch*: *Cath Raon Ruaridh* (The Battle of Killiecrankie), pp.194–5.

6   J. Dalyell and J. Beveridge, 'Inventory of the Plenishing of the House of the Binns at the Date of the Death of General Thomas Dalyell, 21st August 1683. Edited from the Original Documents in the Family Records', *Proceedings of the Society of Antiquaries of Scotland*, 58 (1924), pp.344–370.

7   Smythe, *Letters of John Grahame of Claverhouse*, p.42.

8   Mackenzie, *Orain Iain Luim, Songs of John, Bard of Keppoch*, pp.172–3.

that the Dougals of Craignish 'all carry the brazen hilted sword and wear the girded plaid'.[9]

The description of Stewart of Balquhidder in 1685 epitomises what the gentlemen of any clan would have been carrying; *Bha fear Inbhir-Slanaidh Air a ghainmhich 'na sheasamh /An deigh ghunna a thaomadh Ann an aodann nam marcach / Sgi ath bhallach air uilinn,/Claidheamh fuileach 'na dheas aimh/ Paidhir dhag air a chruachainn Dol a bhualadh Ghilleasbuig.* (The laird of Inverslany was standing on the sands, having emptied his gun in the face of the horsemen. He carried an embossed shield on his elbow, a bloody sword in his right hand, and a pair of pistols on his hip, as he went forward to strike Archibald).[10]

The swords were perhaps most famously deployed at Killiecrankie in a Highland charge. At Killiecrankie, the Highlanders ran towards the enemy until very close then 'pouering it upon them all att once like a great clap of thounder they threw away their guns and fell in pell-mell among the thickest of them with their brodd swords'.[11] The contrast with Dunkeld was that there the men were unable to charge in the same way, as it was unusually for the Jacobite Risings, a battle in an urban environment and so they were picked off by the Government troops. *Cha b 'ann Ie iomairt nan claidhnean/F'hua ir na Gaidheil an leonadh/ 'S iad nach do chleachd seasamh/An taic balla mar chomhdach/ Mar rinneadh ' n Dunn Chailleann/Thuit na gallain ,' s b e ' m bron e/Bhi ' gan leauadh le luaidhe , 's Gun tilgeadh buachaillean 'bho i* (It was not from the play of swords that the Highlanders were wounded / They were not accustomed to stand against a wall for protection, as was done at Dunkeld / The stalwart young men fell and the cause of my sorrow was that they were felled by bullets from cowherds).[12]

The charge, *a' dolsios* (literally going down) had to be done on sloping ground of which there was no shortage at Killiecrankie. This then gave the Highlanders *cothrom a' bhràighe* (the advantage of the brae).[13] The charge had become an important part of Highland battles when armour had been abandoned for the common soldier in the mid sixteenth century, and had been developed into the form that was used at Killiecrankie by Alasdair MacColla some 40 years before during the Civil Wars. 'The Highland men to Advance on us like mad Men, without either shoe or stoking, covering themselves with their Targes, at last they cast away their Musquets, drew their Broad Swords and advanced furiously upon us, and were in the middle of us before we could Fire Three Shots a-piece, broke us, and obliged us to Retreat.'[14] As can be seen from the quote here, MacColla also encouraged

---

9   Murdoch and Philip, *The Grameid*, p.126.

10 *Latha Chearm Loch-Fine* (The Day of the battle at the Head of Loch Fyne), by Alexander Robertson of Bohespic.

11 *Memoirs of Lochiel*, quoted in Mackenzie, *Orain Iain Luim, Songs of John, Bard of Keppoch*, p.310.

12 *Aonghus Mac Alasdair Ruaidh*, quoted in Maclean, 'The Sources, particularly the Celtic Sources, for the History of the Highlands in the Seventeenth Century', p.316.

13 Fforde, *A Lochaber Summer*, p.124.

14 J.J.H.H. Stewart-Murray, Duke of Atholl, and J. Anderson, *Chronicles of the Atholl and Tullibardine Families* (Edinburgh: privately printed, 1908), p.602.

another change that became vital in Highland warfare, the incorporation of guns. The men would run down the hill, the clan gentlemen and tacksmen in the front; then they would fire a volley when they were reasonably close to their enemy, throw down their guns and continue towards to the government troops with sword in hand. Mackay said: 'they come on slowly till they be within distance of firing, which because they keep no rank or file, doth ordinarily little harm. When their fire is over, they throw away their firelocks, and everyone drawing a long broadsword, with his targe (such as have them) on his left hand, they fall a running toward the enemy.'[15]

Philip described 'the muskets thunder and discharge with mighty crash their balls of livid lead'.[16] Martin also says that 'the chief of each Tribe advances within shot of the enemy, having first laid aside their upper Garments; and after one general Discharge, they attack them sword in hand, having their target on their left hand (as they did at Kilicranky)'.[17]

Not every man in the Highland charge had a gun, but those who did were at the front. Many of the guns that were used were those that had been bought for sport or brought from mainland Europe and it is possible that some were from the recent rebellion against James VII led by the Duke of Argyll. Other men in the ranks further back carried Lochaber axes described by Philip as 'hard axe with keen point' or pikes 'other gleaming javelin' and 'knotty clubs'.[18]

The Irish dragoons were for the most part armed with pikes. The average ratio of pikemen to musketeer in conventional armies at this time was still quite high on average perhaps 2:1.[19] This was to fall very swiftly after this campaign as the use of socket bayonets became more popular and those with guns could effectively act as their own pikemen.

It is quite likely that some men at Killiecrankie had bows and Philip mentions 'iron-tipped stakes with keen point,' although the last host of archers of any size in Scotland is likely to have been Lochiel's 'quivered Numidians' when he fought Mackintosh in 1665, 20 years or so before.[20] Dalyell's inventory has two quivers with arrows and seven bows which does possibly suggest the intent to do more than hunt.

The dirk was also an important part of their equipment, 'theirs too was the dirk'. 'James Malcolm deponed that he saw a young lad, called the captain of Clan Ranald, in Lochaber in arms with my Lord Dundee, and that he had a dirk.'[21] It was used in the final part of the Highland charge and it is likely that some of the swords that are described as being of the hands of the Highlanders during this campaign were actually dirks. Burt says that 'the blade is straight and generally above a foot long' and that 'in a close

---

15 Mackay, et al., *Memoirs of the War Carried on in Scotland and Ireland*, p.51.
16 Murdoch and Philip, *The Grameid*, p.214.
17 Martin, *A Description of the Western Islands of Scotland* (1716), p.210.
18 Murdoch and Philip, *The Grameid*, p.129.
19 D. Blackmore, *Destructive and Formidable: British Infantry Firepower 1642–1765* (London: Frontline Books, 2014), p.125.
20 Cheape, *Periods in Highland History*; Murdoch and Philip. *The Grameid*, p.156.
21 Murdoch and Philip. *The Grameid*, pp.126, 156

Plate 1: (Top) Highland Chief, 1715; (Bottom) Highland Man, 1689.
(Illustration by Seán Ó Brógain © Helion & Company 2020)
See Colour Plate Commentaries for further information.

Plate 2: (Top) Trooper, the Royal Regiment of Scots horse 1689; (Bottom) Lowland Officer 1689.
(Illustration by Seán Ó Brógain © Helion & Company 2020)
See Colour Plate Commentaries for further information.

Plate 3: Lowland Levy, 1715.
(Illustration by Seán Ó Brógain © Helion & Company 2020)
See Colour Plate Commentaries for further information.

Plate 4: Spanish infantryman, 1719.
(Illustration by Seán Ó Brógain © Helion & Company 2020)
See Colour Plate Commentaries for further information.

Plate 5: (Top) Flag of the Appin Stewarts; (Bottom) The Lion Rampant – the Royal Standard.
(Illustration by Mark Allen © Helion & Company 2020)
See Colour Plate Commentaries for further information.

Plate 6: (Top) Flag of Nicholas Purcell's Regiment; (Bottom) Flag of Cameron of Lochiel.
(Illustration by Mark Allen © Helion & Company 2020)
See Colour Plate Commentaries for further information.

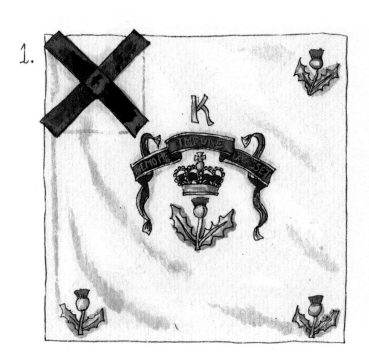

Plate 7: (Top) Flag of Spalding of Glenkilry; (Bottom) Thistle Banner.
(Illustration by Mark Allen © Helion & Company 2020)
See Colour Plate Commentaries for further information.

Plate 8 : (Top) The green banner of Clan Macpherson; (Bottom) The arms of the Duke of Gordon as carried by the Gordons of Strathavan. (Illustration by Mark Allen © Helion & Company 2020)
See Colour Plate Commentaries for further information.

encounter there is no defence'.[22] The decoration on the pommel and the hilt on the dirk had developed during the century. The blade was sometimes an old sword blade cut down. Seventeenth-century dirks usually have small hilts with wide, flat-topped pommels. Most dirks of this period had two bands of ornament, mostly Celtic in style. Into the eighteenth century the grip of the hilt was generally completely carved, it was often studded with brass nails and was deeper. There were some dirks that had hilts of brass or bone [although these seem to have been quite rare in the early part of the century] as well as the more common wood.

There were rumours that a vessel that sailed from Ireland to the Highlands with '6000 stand at arms was forced by stress of weather on our western coast at a place called salt-coats near Irvin is seized.[23] However, these guns do not seem have materialised. Additionally, those that had been regular soldiers did have guns – the garrison at the castle and Dundee's troops. Edinburgh Castle was held in the name of the King. However all the garrison did was 'set up King James's Standard, and give the ordinary vollies of Cannon, which he desired them not to fear, or mistake, and accordingly he fired the Cannon without Bullets, but not without fear to those that lie at the mercy of his Cannon'.[24] The Duke of Gordon had only 120 men, with no trained gunners and many of the arms that might have been expected to have been found in the castle had already been moved to Stirling to equip the Williamite forces. The guns of the castle did however inflict some damage on Edinburgh and some people were killed. 'There was 'great shooting' on both sides, and several were killed, though not many'.[25]

The men from Dundee's troop carried carbines as well as a sword and pistols. The carbine was carried in a sling which was worn over the left shoulder and their sword was carried on the right in a baldric. The flintlock pistols would have been in holsters with yellow holster caps and the housings would also have been yellow.[26] The horse had been issued with armour on their excursion to England, so given that they had to return it before going home; it is likely it was just the officers who had a helmet, a cuirass and a bridle gauntlet as Dundee had.[27] 'Bu mhor cosgradh do lamh/ Fo aon chlogaide ban/'S do chorp nochdaidh geal dan eideadh ai (Wearing your white helmet you wrought great slaughter single-handed and now your naked body lies white and shameless and all unclothed)'.[28] The Grameid has several references to armour, some of which are so self-consciously Homeric as to be unlikely however many others seem some plausible: Fraser of Lovat has 'heavy armour on his shoulder; another chief is described as 'conspicuous in shining armour and Lochiel 'fiercely dons his armour'.[29] To get an idea of the

---

22 Burt, *Burt's Letters*, p.174.
23 Balfour-Melville, *An Account of the Proceedings of the Estates in Scotland, 1689–1690*, p.47.
24 Colin Lindsay, Earl of Balcarres, *Memoirs Touching the Revolution in Scotland* (Edinburgh: Bannatyne Club, 1841), p.20.
25 Balfour-Melville, *An Account of the Proceedings of the Estates in Scotland, 1689–1690*, p.22.
26 Ede-Borrett, *The Army of James II*, pp.43–44.
27 Ede-Borrett, *The Army of James II*, p.44.
28 Iain Lom – the Battle of Killecrankie.
29 Murdoch and Philip, *The Grameid*, pp.150, 152, 132.

kind of weapons that many of those volunteering to fight for Dundee would have been carrying, on the other side the resolutely Williamite, Sir John Foulis lent 'ye Gardiner James Orr and Ja. Blackader – a musket, a carabine, 2 broadswords a belt and a pair of bandeliers'.[30] He also bought 'half a pund of powder' which cost him 10s and a dozen each of pistol and carabine balls at two and three shillings respectively.[31] Not all of the men fighting would have been as well armed.

Colonel Dalyell had in his inventory in 1688, 'an instrument of timber for casting ball, four pair of hulster pistols (for use on horseback); three pairs of iron pistols and a black leather bag wherein is ane embroyed patrontasch'.[32] The patrontasch would be one solution to carrying cartridges (or patrons as they were called in Scots) for his guns. The Williamite army ordered large numbers of them in 1689 however they seem to have had some difficulty in paying for them so it is debatable how many of the cartridge boxes which were worn with a belt would have been out in the field immediately.[33] The capacity of these boxes was limited and would have been supplemented by powder horns. In the contemporary portrait of Lord Mungo Murray, he had two pistols in his waist belt with gold prickers. He also had a powder horn and three brass powder measures. Each of those would have contained a measured charge which could be poured down the barrel of his pistol. A bag containing the musket balls was also necessary and many soldiers kept the balls in their mouths and spat the lead balls down the barrel of the gun to speed up loading.[34]

Dundee struggled to obtain enough powder, having only around 50 pounds 'When we came first out, I had but fifty pounds of powder; more I could not get; all the great towns and sea-ports were in rebellion, and had seized the powder, and would sell none. But I had one advantage, the Highlanders will not fire above once, and then take to the broad-sword.'[35]

Some of the Jacobites were carrying the more old-fashioned and clumsier to use snaphaunces rather than the more up to date dog lock muskets that certainly some of the gentry would have been carrying since they were used not only for sport as well as military purposes. However, the snaphaunce muskets had been so ubiquitous that gunmakers in the early part of the century were sometimes called snapmakers and as late as 1718 'there were sent … to the magazines of Edinburgh castle three hundered and fifty snaphans'.[36]

---

30 Hallen, *The Account Book of Sir John Foulis of Ravelston*, p.109.
31 Hallen, *The Account Book of Sir John Foulis of Ravelston*, p.108.
32 Dalyell, J., and Beveridge, J., 'Inventory of the Plenishing of the House of the Binns at the Date of the Death of General Thomas Dalyell, 21st August 1683. Edited from the Original Documents in the Family Records', *Proceedings of the Society of Antiquaries of Scotland* 58 (1924), pp.344–370.
33 'Patrontas(c)h(e) *n*.'. *Dictionary of the Scots Language* (online), 2004. Scottish Language Dictionaries Ltd. <https://dsl.ac.uk/entry/dost/patrontasch>, accessed 5 April 2019.
34 Blackmore, *Destructive and Formidable*, p.29.
35 Smythe, *Letters of John Grahame of Claverhouse*, p.47.
36 'Snaphaunce, *n*.'. *Dictionary of the Scots Language* (online) 2004. Scottish Language Dictionaries Ltd. <https://dsl.ac.uk/entry/dost/snaphaunce>, accessed 25 June 2019.

'They began to descend and having made a ragged fire threw away their snaphans, and ran down the hill with drawn broad-swords and targes.'[37] Mackay had 'commanded the officers, commanding battalions to begin their firing at 100 paces by platoons, to discourage the Highlanders meeting with continual fire'.[38]

A manual written by the Williamite general, Sir Thomas Livingston in 1693, advised:

> The Musket must lie upon the Left Shoulder, and the Left Hand upon the Butt-end, the Thumb in the Hollow thereof, pressing the Guard hard against the Breast, that the Muzzel of the Musket may be mounted; the Lock must be turn'd a little outwards, so that the under Part of the Butt-end come straight with the middle of the Body, that the Musket may more easily be born.[39]

Flintlocks in general had become more popular; on the Williamite side the Laird of Grant's men all had flintlocks.[40] It appears however that MacDonald of Glencoe was using a blunderbuss. 'James Malcolm depones, that "he sawe a man called the Laird of Glencoe in armes with the rebells at Badenoch, Strathspey, and severall other places, and that he had a brasse blunderbus, and a buff coat".'[41] Additionally, 'the young laird of Innercy, his father having fallen & after being left for dead on the place, after three or four hours stay amongst the dead bodies & whilst our men were in pursuit of the Rebels, made shift to get up & make his escape, leaving his head piece, target, blunderbuss & other arms.'[42] This also suggests he was wearing a helmet (head-piece). Philip described MacDonald of Glencoe as being 'covered as to his breast with raw hide' and the Macleods of Raasay as wearing 'oxhide tunics' while this sounds exotic they were actually buff coats.[43]

'Many officers and soldiers were cut down through the skull and neck to the very breasts others had skulls cut off above the ears … some had both their bodies and their cross belts cut through at one blow, pikes and small swords were cut like willows.'[44] The bloody horror of the descriptions of the slaughter at Killiecrankie does make it clear that while Dundee's army might have used guns initially, they finished their killing with swords, dirks and pikes. *Is iomadh bearraid is gruag/ Bha 'gan spealtadh mu'n cnuac/ Bha fuil*

37 Mackay and Bannatyne Club, *The Life of Lieut.-General Hugh Mackay of Scoury*, p.153.

38 Mackay, et al., *Memoirs of the War Carried on in Scotland and Ireland*, p.50.

39 *The exercise of the foot with the evolutions, according to the words of command, as they are explained: as also the forming of battalions, with directions to be observed by all colonels, captains and other officers in His Majesties armies. Likewise, the exercise of the dragoons both on horse-back and foot. With the rules of war in the day of battel, when encountering the enemy, ordered by Sir Thomas Livingston, Major General, and commander in chief of their Majesties forces in Scotland. Recommended to all (officers as well as souldiers) in their Majesties armies.* (1693)

40 S. Reid, *The Flintlock Musket, Brown Bess and Charleville 1715–1865* (Oxford: Osprey Publishing, 2016), p.28.

41 Stewart, *Old and Rare Scottish Tartans*, p.112.

42 Stewart, *Old and Rare Scottish Tartans*, p.112.

43 Murdoch and Philip, *The Grameid*, pp.124, 146.

44 Hill, *Celtic Warfare*, p.64.

dhaithte 'na stuaigh air feur a muigh (Many a cocked hat and periwig was being smashed on their pates / red blood flowed in waves over the grass on the field);[45] or *Ach gur lionmhor ad ' rachta Bha mu 'heata Raon- Ruairidh / Agus Gaidheal gun bhreacan A ' ruithe fir casaige ruaidhe.* (But numerous were the crushed skulls that lay about the gate of Raon-Ruairidh / as plaidless Highlanders chased the red cassocks).[46] In Lochiel's Memoirs the slaughter is described as 'Many had their heads divided into two halves by one blow; others had their sculls cut off above the eares by a back-strock like a night-cap.'[47]

---

45 MacKenzie, *Orain Iain Luim, Songs of John, Bard of Keppoch*: *Cath RaonRuaridh* (The Battle of Killiecrankie) pp.194–5.

46 *Aonghus Mac Alasdair Ruaidh*, quoted in Maclean, 'The Sources, particularly the Celtic Sources, for the History of the Highlands in the Seventeenth Century'.

47 MacKenzie, *Orain Iain Luim, Songs of John, Bard of Keppoch, Memoirs of Locheil* p.271 quoted p.313.

4

When every brave hero will rise in his splendid new uniform

Is i seo an aimsir an dearbhar an tairgneach dhuinn,
Is bras meanmnach Fir Alban fo an armaibh air thùs.
An uair a dh'èireas gach treun laoch 'n éideadh glan ùr,
Le rùn feirge agus gairge gu seirbhis a' Chrùin.
'This is the time when the Prophecy will be proved for us,
The Men of Scotland are keen and spirited under arms and at
the forefront of battle.
When every brave hero will rise in his splendid new uniform,
In a mood of anger and fierceness for the service of the Crown.'

Earl of Mar
Lieutenant General : Cullen, Ecklin, Fraser George Hamilton
Major Generals: Thomas Buchan, Gordon of Auchintoul
Brigadier Generals: Campbell, Corbet, Lord Drummond, Mackintosh of
    Borlam
Marquess of Huntly, Viscount Kenmure, Marquess of Seaforth, Marquess of
    Tullibardine Foot
Major General Gordon of Auchintoul

Brigades
Huntly's Brigade:
Glenbuchat's Regiment
Leith Regiment
Innes
Macphersons
Glenbuchat's horse squadron
Sinclair Horse squadron
1st, 2nd & 3rd horse Huntly horse
Seaforth Brigade – five battalions plus two horse troops
Applecross
Fairbairn
Ballmackie and McKeldin

Fraser and Chisholm
MacDonald of Sleat
Seaforth Horse troop
Tulibardine's brigades
Lord Nairne's Regiment's
Lord Charles Murray's Regiment
Atholl Brigade – eight battalions
Inverey
Thomas Drummond of Logiealmond
Ogilvy
Lord Panmure
Stewart of Invernytie
Strathmore
Strathallan[1]

In 1715 Rising, there was far greater popular support than there had been in 1689/90. The biggest cause of this change was the Union of the Parliaments between Scotland and England. There had been pro-Jacobite and anti-Union demonstrations in much of Scotland in the years before the Rising. When the Earl of Mar raised his standard at Braemar then men from all over Scotland came. Indeed in Perth on 1 October 1715 the army was described as 'betwixt three and four thousand foot … and all in Highland cloaths tho mostly Lowland men' – as can be seen from the list of the men recruited this was not entirely true however there was a much wider geographical spread to those who fought for the Jacobites in 1715 than there had been previously including many from the north-east and Perthshire.[2] Eventually there were almost 10 times as many men in the field for the '15 as there had been in 1689. Many of those who were fighting wore Highland garb although only approximately one third of the army was Highland, for example in Lord Panmure's battalion all of the men wore Highland clothes, except for Strathmore's regiment. Over the years since 1689 the wearing of tartan and Highland garb had for many become a political act and statement of support for the Stuarts. Lord Charles Murray wore Highland dress to encourage his men; 'upon all marches, he could never be prevailed with to ride, but kept to the head of his regiment on foot in, his Highland dress without Breeches'.[3]

The mainstay of the 'Highland cloaths' was of course the plaid. This was little changed since 1689 although the growing ease of importation of dyestuffs meant that the bright colours that were so popular among the Highland elite in particular could be more simply obtained. It would be a mistake however to assume that even plebeian men in the relatively isolated Highlands and certainly elsewhere in Scotland were not increasingly aware of changes in fashion and consumption and therefore affected by them.

---

1   Pittock, *The Myth of the Jacobite Clans*, pp.187–90; J. Oates, *The Crucible of the Jacobite '15: The Battle of Sheriffmuir 1715* (Solihull: Helion & Company, 2017), pp.50–1, 108.
2   M. Pittock, *The Myth of the Jacobite Clans* (Edinburgh: Edinburgh University Press, 2015), pp.39-40.
3   Quoted in Oates, *The Crucible of the Jacobite '15*, p.120.

Kenneth Sutherland, 3rd Lord Duffus, by Richard Waitt. Lord Duffus took part in the 1715 Rising. However, this painting was done before he joined in the Jacobites in approximately 1712. He is dressed for hunting as many of those who attended Mar's tincel at the start of the 1715 Rising would have been. His plaid is brown, yellow with red and white stripes. He is wearing a dirk with a plain handle and two smaller knives or possibly a knife and fork tucked in the sheath. He has a ramshorn pistol in his belt and powder horn. His red jacket is slashed as Philip described in *The Grameid* to show the full sleeves of his very white linen shirt. His hose are made of a different tartan to his plaid and worn with colourful garters. His shoes have a decorated tongue and toe. (Image © National Galleries of Scotland)

Stewart of Garth in the early nineteenth century sought to find out what the older patterns of tartan might be, he received this answer from Col. Alexander Robertson of Struan: 'More than twenty years ago I wished to ascertain what the pattern of Clandonachy Tartan was , and applied to different old men of the Clan for information … but no two descriptions I received were exactly the similar, and they were all very vulgar and gaudy',[4] This rather sounds like the descriptions may have been for older patterns since they were very bright. Lord James Murray took three highland plaids with him along with a great many other things and Laurence Oliphant took 'Blankets or Hyland plaids',[5] Lord Charles Nairn, 'always went with them on Foot through the worst and deepest ways, and in Highland dress'.[6] Reports of Mar's army describe them in September 1715 as 'in Highland Habits, With swords, pistols and targets and some had firelocks'.[7] There were no clan chiefs or Colonels in 1715 who dressed their men like the Whig Laird of Grant 'for his 'hosting or hunteing'; each man was to be dressed in 'Heighland coates, trewes, and short hoes of Tartane of red and greine sett broad springed and also with gun, sword, pistoll and durk'.[8] Although the tenants of the Marquess of Huntly in the parishes of Rhynie, Kinoir, Cairnie, Ruthven, and Gairtly provided plaids, tartan, hose, swords and guns.[9] The Earl Marischal had 'bought up and dyed great parcels of cloath for soldiers cloathes. This is reported by those who sold the Cloath and spoke with the man who dyed it'.[10] Like the Laird of Grant's men a few years before the Rising, many of the gentlemen who fought would have been wearing trews. Lord James Murray or possibly Lord Tullibardine since it is actually likely these were his belongings, had two pairs of 'trues' and five pairs of garters including two of highland garters like those worn by Lord Duffus.[11]

Intriguingly he also has a pair of tartan breeches listed and it is difficult to know if these were in fact trews, which is the most likely explanation or if unusually they are actually breeches made in tartan. Trews which are described by Martin as being 'fine woven like Stockings of those cloth; some are colour'd and other striped; the latter are as well shap'd as the former lying close to the body'.[12] Trews were often gartered as contemporary portraits show for the example the splendid portrait of Major Fraser of Castle Leathers, or the posthumous portrait of Andrew MacPherson of Cluny which was painted in the early 1720s.

---

4 J. Robertson, *The First Highlander: Major-general David Stewart of Garth CB, 1768–1829* (East Linton: Tuckwell, 1998), p.75.
5 Kington-Oliphant, *The Jacobite Lairds of Gask*, p.28.
6 Quoted in Oates, *The Crucible of the Jacobite '15*, p.120.
7 Quoted in Oates, *The Crucible of the Jacobite '15*, p.123.
8 Stewart, *Old and Rare Scottish Tartans*, pp.27–8.
9 GD44/51/167/4 – list of materiel and men provided by tenants in parishes of Rhynie, Kinoir, Cairnie, Ruthven, Gairtly, Dunbennan and in Raws of Huntly.
10 A. Tayler and H. Tayler, *1715: The Story of the Rising* (London, New York: T. Nelson, 1936), p.30. Unfortunately, there is no information on colours or what sort of clothing, however 'cloath' used in this context implies the strong possibility that Marischal's men might have had matching coats.
11 Stewart-Murray and Anderson, *Chronicles of the Atholl and Tullibardine Families*, p.cviii.
12 Martin, *A Description*, p.207.

Andrew Macpherson of Cluny, by Richard Waitt. The clothes that Macpherson of Cluny is wearing would be much like those worn by Highland officers at Sheriffmuir. The trews, with scarlet garters, are of green and brown tartan; the pattern of the jacket with slashed sleeves is different to that of the plaid which has a red stripe. He is wearing square-toed shoes with a small buckle. He has a targe and a pair of pistols laid on top of a blue bonnet and is wearing a basket-hilted broadsword. (Image © National Galleries of Scotland)

The garters and a belt would help with the fit of the trews and stop them from falling down as Martin describes 'tied round with a belt above the haunches'. It is perfectly possible particularly given the time of year that many of the men in the campaign wore both as in Burt's illustrations from the 1720s where men can be seen wearing both a belted plaid and trews. Trews at this point would have had a button fly, the fall front being a later addition. Martin describes the 'square piece of cloth which hangs down before – this can be clearly seen in some contemporary depictions.[13]

Rob Roy and his men in 1716 occupied the palace of Falkland, most likely under the orders of Jacobite high command.[14] It was likely that his plan was to raid the country and destroy any forage that might be there for horses, although forage in winter time in Scotland was always a problem. He and his body of about 150 Highlanders 'robs and plunder taking cloaths and vituals'.[15]

The inventory from the Atholl chronicles lists nine plain shirts and eight shirts with' lace at the breast'. Clean, white linen was the mark of respectability and gentility. A gentleman might expect to change his shirt several times a day. Laurence Oliphant took 18 fine shirts with him and another 'three of coarse linnen' as well as three nightshirts. Shirts in the late 1600s and early 1700s worn by Highlanders had very full sleeves and required several yards of linen. At this time, linen produced in Scotland was generally quite a coarse fabric.[16] The finest linen came from Holland hence the frequent descriptions of shirts, handkerchiefs or cravats as 'two Holland handkerchiefs' or George Home in 1694 who had '2 Holland shirts'.[17] Some of the poorer men may well have been wearing wool shirts like those found on the bog bodies at Arnish Moor and Gunnister and possibly no breeches as the body was found without any. The Arnish Moor man was wearing two wool shirts.[18] Wool shirts were not popular in England at this time partly because Charles II had introduced an act of Parliament which made it compulsory to be buried in wool and they had come therefore to be regarded as old-fashioned and unhealthy.[19] It is likely that some of the men would have been wearing 'halfe-shirts' underneath their shirts whether wool or linen, these were a short undershirt of linen or sometimes flannel often worn in the winter as an extra layer.[20] George Home had four Holland half shirts, the accounts at Dunvegan show the purchase of 'two halfe shirts' and Sir John Foulis bought 'Holland' for his wife to make halfshirts.

Shirts worn with lowland clothing, might be made with fine, white, and expensive Holland, cambric, lawn or coarser forms of linen dependant on

13 Martin, *A Description of the Western Islands of Scotland*, p.207.
14 D. Stevenson, *The Hunt for Rob Roy: The Man and the Myths* (Edinburgh: Birlinn, 2016), p.118.
15 Stevenson, *The Hunt for Rob Roy*, p.118.
16 See Tuckett, 'Weaving the Nation'.
17 Wilcox, 'Scottish Late Seventeenth-Century Male Clothing', pp.150–162.
18 Wilcox, 'Scottish Late Seventeenth-Century Male Clothing (Part 2)', pp.28–53.
19 'Charles II, 1677 & 1678: An Act for burying in Woollen', J. Styles, *The Dress of the People: Everyday Fashion in Eighteenth-Century England* (New Haven: Yale University Press, 2007), p.24.
20 Cunnington and Willet, *The History of Underclothes*, p.58.

social standing and money. The bottom of the shirt was cut square with splits up the side. The sleeves were cut generously. The whiteness of the linen reflected the cleanliness of the person wearing it, or so it was believed therefore the whiter the linen – the cleaner and more respectable the wearer was presumed to be. Therefore, the chances of presenting a respectable figure were increased by owning as many shirts as possible. White linen however required upkeep and someone to wash it. From 1710 onwards the hanging cravat as worn by Dundee and his officers of the previous century was worn infrequently and the frilled or laced part of the shirt (like those owned by Tullibardine) was more on display. The *Spectator* of July 1711 described 'his new silk waistcoat which was unbuttoned in several places to let us see that he had a clean shirt on which was ruffled to his middle'.[21] In addition to a clean shirt, ruffles, and cravats were a means by which wealth and cleanliness, could be further displayed since they could be detached and were fairly easily washed. The Murray inventory has a large number of cravats: 40 travelling cravats; 15 muslean cravats; 4 cravats bound with lace and 17 camrick (cambric)[22] cravats. In contrast Oliphant took a relatively modest 18 cravats with him. Murray also has 16 pairs of muslin ruffles. The Macleods at Dunvegan bought laced cravats and several pairs of sleeves.[23] In 1712, the laird of Gask gave John Coldstream, a schoolmaster, 'sum of twentie five pounds eighteen shillings & six pence Scots for mounting William Oliphant in Coat, Vest, Breeches, Shirts, Cravats, and all necessary Aboulziements (garments).[24] Plebeian men wore simpler versions of elite clothing. The coat found with the Gunnister man has many details on that ape those of fashions further up the social scale including the pockets on the coat fronts, and its buttons. These details of the Gunnister coat, made in the style of a fashionable coat but in heavy, hard-wearing wool date it to the end of the seventeenth century, so common men during the first Jacobite Rising and older men in the second who were not wearing Highland clothes are likely to have been wearing something similar to this.[25] This coat had wool buttons which onwards can be seen particularly on plebeian clothing from the late medieval period which can be seen be seen particularly on plebeian clothing from the late medieval period onwards.

Under their coats, most men wore a waistcoat or vest as it was often called at the time. Burt says that the waistcoats worn with Highland clothes were 4 or 5 inches (10.1–12.7cm) longer than the short highland coat.[26] Murray had a 'highland coat and vest lined with whit silk'. In the previous century there had been attempts to control the importation of silk into Scotland in

21 Cunnington and Willet, *The History of Underclothes*, p.75.
22 J.J.J.H. Stewart-Murray, Duke of Atholl, and J. Anderson, *Chronicles of the Atholl and Tullibardine Families* (Edinburgh: privately printed, 1908), p.20.
23 MacLeod, *The Book of Dunvegan*, pp.207–8.
24 T.L. Kington-Oliphant, *The Jacobite Lairds of Gask* (London, Published for the Grampian Club by C. Griffin & Co., 1870), p.20-22.
25 Older people often clung to the fashions of their youth, so there tended to be a bit of a time lag with the clothing worn by those over 40 or so. This was less common in the elite, naturally. See Wilcox, 'Scottish Late Seventeenth-Century Male Clothing (Part 2)', pp.28–53.
26 Burt, *Burt's Letters*, p.231.

order to encourage manufacture with Scotland, these efforts had ceased on the Union. Colin Campbell of Glenure in his list of moveable goods some years after the Rising, had 'Highland cloaths and short westcoats'.[27] Murray also owned waistcoats or vests that were for wearing with Lowland clothes including; one strip fustian vest (fustian was a mixed fabric, generally linen and cotton). Fustian was very popular among working men so many of those in the army would have had something similar. Coats and waistcoats generally matched but white waistcoats were common for informal wear, and flannel waistcoats were often worn for warmth. Knitted waistcoats had been popular in seventeenth century for both men and women but by the turn of the century were very old fashioned.

With a belted plaid men generally wore short hose made from tartan although the finds at both Arnish Moor and Barrock Estate had short cloth hose associated generally with Lowland style clothing.[28] Those dressed in Lowland fashion would have been wearing knee-length breeches made commonly generally from dark coloured wool 'breeches of cloath' as listed in the Atholl inventory. Leather breeches would also have been a common choice throughout the time period. The majority of the leather for them would have been brought from North America since Europe had stopped being self-sufficient in buckskin during the sixteenth century. Leather breeches were practical and hard wearing and worn across the social classes. Breeches at this time were generally fastened with two buttons, one above the other as in the seventeenth century. They often had pockets.

For the most part men wearing breeches would be wearing knitted stockings. In Scotland, these were generally hand knitted, often in Aberdeenshire. There had been an act of Parliament in 1664 'For instructing of the poore children, vagabounds and other idlers to fine and mix wooll, spin worstead and knit stockings'. George Pyper in Aberdeenshire paid his knitters five groats (one groat was fourpence) a pair but some were so fine he 'hath given twenty shillings sterling and upwards for a pair'.[29] There had also been an attempt to set up stocking frame knitters as in England however despite the importation of several men and machines this did not prove to be successful until later in the century. Although a few years before 1715 an advertisement appeared for a shop 'in the luckenbooths at the Poll and Stockens above the Old Kirck-Style' in Edinburgh where Andrew Cockburn 'having his care and industry improves his stocken manufactory better than any other in the kingdom, sells all sorts of silk, silk and worsted, and finist worsted stockens'.[30] Stockings were usually knitted out of worsted yarn. Blue, white and black were the most common colours although sheep's black (from the natural colour of darker sheep's wool); clouded (made from mixing two colours), grey and brown were also popular. Tullibardine had three pairs

---

27 S. Nenadic, 'The Highlands of Scotland in the First Half of the Eighteenth Century: Consuming at a Distance', *British Journal for Eighteenth-Century Studies*, 28 (2005), pp.215–228.

28 Wilcox, 'Scottish Late Seventeenth-Century Male Clothing (Part 2)', pp.28–53.

29 Chambers, *Domestic Annals of Scotland*.

30 C. Gulvin, *The Scottish Hosiery and Knitwear Industry 1680–1980* (Edinburgh: Donald, 1984), p.12.

of worsted stockings and the same number of silk stockings as well as one pair of scarlet stockings. Sir John Foulis bought a pair of new black of worsit stockings in 1704 for £3 12 Scots. Oliphant had three pairs of silk stockings and one pair of Kilmarnock (knitted) stockings in his packing for the Rising.[31]

The shoes that men wore with highland dress had changed little since 1689 however although in England gentry men or indeed men with pretensions to respectability would not by 1715 have owned boots that were not riding boots; this does not seem to have been the case in Scotland. Tullibardine had one pair of boots, nine pairs of shoes – although inconsiderately what sort of type is not listed. Sir John Foulis in 1679 spent £14 on a new pair of black boots and £14 10s on black 'shoes and galashoes'. In 1725, Alexander Campbell, an advocate and commissary of the artillery at Edinburgh Castle, owned two pairs of shoes, a pair of slippers, and three pairs of boots.[32]

Many ordinary men in the Highlands wore their hair long in contrast to the fashion which was to cut the hair very short and then wear a wig. Gentry and professional men would have tended to have worn a wig and in the Lowlands, as in England. Wig wearing was very common across the social classes. For example, John Mork, a candlemaker from Edinburgh who died in 1718 had a 'hatt and a wigg'.[33] Oliphant took a 'box with weegs, pouder and ouyle' [the powder and oil were for dressing the wigs]. Tullibardine also took 'one Weig in a box'.[34]

Most of the men in highland dress would have been wearing a knitted bonnet, blue for the most part. 'The highland gentlemen were mighty civil, dress'd in their short slash'd waistcoats, a trousing (which is, breeches and stockings of one piece of strip'd stuff) with a plaid for a cloak and a blue bonnet'.[35] The Atholl inventory has '2 blue bonnets' listed.[36] On their bonnets and hats many Jacobites in this Rising wore a white cockade. White had long been a colour associated with the Stuarts. Sympathisers had worn the white rose during the Exclusion crisis since York's badge was the white rose but this does not seem to carried forward into a badge for the Jacobites until the 1700s. In 1713, a parade ostensibly in honour of Queen Anne had men with 'a cockade of white Ribbon on their hats'. In August 1714 'some ill disposed persons in Aberdeen Did at night and under the cover of womens' apparell, proclaim the pretender'.[37] In 1714, white gloves with the word 'liberty' on them were sold in Edinburgh.[38] In 1715, James Watson, a journey printer was charged with wearing 'a cockade in his hat' on 10 June (James VIII's birthday); in London Jacobite sympathisers were 'making a Bonfire, ringing

---

31 A.W.C. Hallen, *The Account Book of Sir John Foulis of Ravelston*, p.185.

32 Tuckett, 'Weaving the Nation', p.85.

33 Nenadic, 'Necessities: Food and Clothing in the Long Eighteenth Century'.

34 T.L. Kington-Oliphant, *The Jacobite Lairds of Gask*, p.20; Stewart-Murray and Anderson, *Chronicles of the Atholl and Tullibardine Families*, p.cviii

35 Quote in Stewart, *Old and Rare Scottish Tartans*, p.29.

36 Stewart-Murray and Anderson, *Chronicles of the Atholl and Tullibardine Families*, p.cviii.

37 J. Allardyce (ed.), *Historical Papers Relating to the Jacobite Period, 1699–1750*, 2 vols (Aberdeen: 1895, 1896), vol. I, 28. Although it should be noted that feminising your opponents was a particularly good way of neutralising their threat.

38 Pittock, *Material culture and Sedition*, pp.74–5.

the Bells in White-Chappel, and strolling about of several scoundrels with cockades in their hats.'[39]

Thomas Morer in 1689 wrote about the Scots' love for tobacco and particularly snuff. Although smoking was pretty much endemic everywhere and clay pipes could be bought with a single charge of tobacco in them and then were often discarded afterward hence why there are often so many of them found in any archaeological dig of this period.

> They are fond of Tobacco, but more from the Snush-Box than Pipe. And they have made it so necessary, that I have heard some of 'em say, That should their Bread come in competition with it, they would rather Fast than their Snush should be taken away. Yet mostly it consists of the coursest Tobacco, dried by the Fire, and powdered in a little Engine after the form of a Tap, which they carry in their Pockets, and is both a Mill to grind, and a Box to keep it in.[40]

His observations were confirmed by John Loveday in 1732. He noted he had not seen a smoker or a pipe in Scotland, 'yet they consume vast quantities of Tobacco, for there are None from ye richest to ye poorest but Who take Snuff at a most immoderate rate'.[41] Thanks in part to this addiction to snuff, a mill had become an important part of the Highlanders' dress. It was fastened at the belt and worn like a purse in front of the plaid. In the Outer Hebrides the men chewed their tobacco rather than smoke it or take snuff and kept it in leather bags made of sealskin. These bags were called 'spleuchans' and kept the tobacco soft and tasty. Pedlars carried small packets of tobacco and tea to even the most remote parts of the Highlands along with buttons, ribbons and small amounts of fabric.[42]

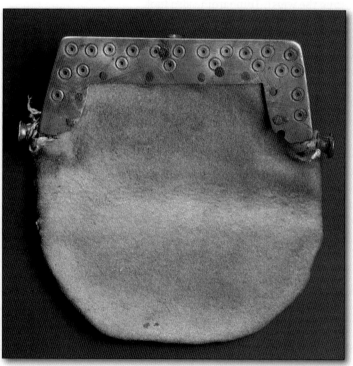

A small eighteenth-century sporran (purse) made from deerskin with a typical rectangular brass cantle. This particular sporran is said to have been owned by Rob Roy MacGregor. (Image © National Museums Scotland)

The sporran or purse, was not yet the huge furry monstrosity that dominates the front of so many Victorian kilts in black and white photographs but a much more practical, if less impressive bag. It was made generally quite simply

---

39 J. Allardyce (ed.), *Historical Papers Relating to the Jacobite Period, 1699–1750*, 2 vols (Aberdeen: 1895, 1896), vol. I, 28. Although it should be noted that feminising your opponents was a particularly good way of neutralising their threat.

40 Hume Brown, *Early travellers in Scotland*, p.263.

41 J. Loveday, *Diary of a tour in 1732 through parts of England, Wales, Ireland and Scotland* (Edinburgh: privately printed, 1890), p.127.

42 Nenadic, *Lairds and Luxury*, p.155.

from deer or calf skin, sometimes seal. Extant examples in the National Museum of Scotland and elsewhere show they could be quite small, not much more than a few inches across, although Major Fraser of Castle Leather in his portrait has a sporran that looks more like a bag and therefore also demonstrates that some were considerably larger. The majority of eighteenth-century sporrans had a brass clasp or cantle, however examples from the 1600s do not have the cantle. Frequently, the front would be incised with a simple design, often concentric circles The bag itself had one central and then two hinge thongs with tassels and was, therefore laced to the clasp with the thongs. The sporran would be divided internally into smaller pockets with a leather partition.

5

Most threw away their fuzies

Gheibhte sud ann ad fhàrdaich
An càradh air ealchainn,
Miosair is adharc
Is rogha gach armachd.
Miosair is adharc
Is rogha gach armachd,
Agus lanntainean tana
O'n ceannaibh gu'm barrdheis.
Gheibhte sud air gach suos dhiubh
Isneach is cairbinn,
(in thy dwelling would be found, ranged
upon the weapon-rack, powder-horn and shot-horn
and the pick of every armoury.,
and sword-blades slender-tapering from hilt to tip;
would be found on each side of them rifle and carabine)[1]

The order to attack being given, the two thousand Highlanders, who were then drawn up in very good order, ran towards the enemie in a disorderlie manner, always fireing some dropeing shots. Which drew upon them a general salvo from enemie which began at their left, opposite us, and turn to their right. No sooner that begun, the Highlanders threw themselves flat on their bellies, and when it slackened, they started to their feet. Most threw away their fuzies, and drawing their swords, pierced them everie where with ane incredible vigour and rapidities … the Highlanders pursued the infantrie who run as hard as their feet could carrie them.[2]

Rumours abounded in the summer of 1715 about the possibility of French involvement in any rising. 'In Angus and further north they talke confidently

---

1   J. Carmichael Watson, *Gaelic Songs of Mary MacLeod* (London: Blackie & Son, 1934), pp.80–1.

2   W. Scott (ed.), *Memoirs of the insurrection in Scotland in 1715* (Edinburgh, 1845), pp.217–8. Fuzies were fusils, a lighter, shorter version of the matchlock originally of a smaller calibre.

that the Duke of Berwick is to Land in Brittain with 15 or 20,000 men.[3] However, the French authorities had made it clear that there would be no overt support for James. James would have to travel through France secretly to reach the channel ports and he would not be given French troops or arms.

'It was also said that James was expected with a French army and would be joined by 12,000 Highlanders as the same again from England and Ireland. Argyle met with Montrose and John Ker, Duke of Roxburghe to discuss how to use the few loyal troops stationed in Scotland if this were to happen.'[4]

The Master of Sinclair who was quite dismissive of his fellow Jacobites suggested that while waiting for James and his sadly elusive army of well-armed Frenchmen or at very least that large number of stand at arms that they hoped for that the best thing they 'could doe in the meantime was provide armes and horses'. He eventually persuaded the other conspirators that in addition to the 'fiftie firelocks' that he had sent to Holland for, they should send Mr Henry Crawford for 'fourscore carabines and carabine belts and as many pistols with a small amount of powder and flints.[5] Despite this Sinclair wrote that some of the men were 'without carabines' and many others only had 'old rustie muskets, who had never fired one in their lives'. Many of the Jacobites were also busy buying horses which might be suitable for military service' at extravagant prices' and 'Mr Lockhart of Carnwath has of late bought many such horses';[6] 'Some privatt gentilmen of the neighbourhood have not under five or six a piece, and I am certain some of them have not money of ther own unless they have a fond from abroad to support the charge they are att.'[7]

Seaforth was 'much employed of late in warlike preparations', having 1,500 men he could call upon. A magazine of arms and ammunition was

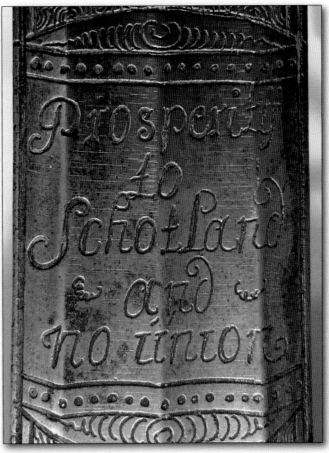

The spelling of Scotland as Schotland demonstrates the German origin of this particular blade. Blades of this type were generally produced pre-Union. (Image © Battle of Falkirk Muir Visitor Centre)

3   D. Szechi, *1715: The Great Jacobite Rebellion* (New Haven: Yale University Press, 2006), p.75. The Duke of Berwick was James' half brother.

4   P. Rae, *A short history of the late rebellion and of the conduct of divine Providence … : in a letter from Edinburgh to a gentleman at Dumfries* (Edinburgh: Printed by Robert Brown, 1716), p.123.

5   Scott, *Memoirs of the insurrection in Scotland in 1715*, pp.17, 40, 189.

6   J. Maidment (ed.), *The Argyle Papers* (Edinburgh: T.G. Stevenson, 1834), p.134, 'Memorial for his Grace of Argyle'.

7   Szechi, *1715: The Great Jacobite Rebellion*, p.95.

being assembled by George Keith, the Earl Marischal as well as uniform and tents.[8] Laurence Oliphant packed a tent bed which implies the expectation of a tent to put it in. Back in the 1680s, Dalyell had a ligour (military) chest and bed which again implies some of sort of expectation of tents being provided when on campaign.

Intelligence reports claimed that there had been 5,000 stand at arms landed at Dunottar in the north-east of Scotland but it is difficult to back this up with solid evidence.[9] In October, Sinclair tried to capture the 3,000 muskets that were reputed to be on board a ship, however when he got there, he was only able to find 'three hundred wanting one' and 'two barrels of musket balls, some flints and two or three barrels of gunpowder at about 100 each'.[10] It was reported that arms had been landed at Aberdour, overlooking the Firth of Forth for Patrick Lyon of Auchterhouse and others in Fife.[11] Summons against the ex Provost of Perth, Patrick Davidson in Perth state that he and others did 'cloathe themselves with weapons and instruments bellical [warlike]'.[12] On 17 October 1715, Mar asked Aberdeen for 300 Lochaber axes to be made and sent to the camp at Perth. On the 23–24 October, orders were made for gunpowder and lead. The lack of powder was a problem so while the Jacobites had some 1,800kg of powder seized at Aberdeen, in December there was 'insufficient for even one day's fighting' at Perth.[13]

One of the problems with preparations for the Rising was that each member of the gentry expected to be able to equip his own men. This obviously made for inconstancies in the preparation since only some were able to turn out well organised and properly armed regiments. The Marquess of Huntly and Lord Panmure had sufficient money and contacts to be able to put together a regiment that was well armed; reports at the end of September suggested that Lord Panmure's battalion were 'armed with Gun, sword Targe and most part side pistol. Sume had Bayonetts'. Huntly had bought 300 horses.[14] By September 1715 there were some attempts to commandeer arms under a commission from Mar. 'These are Ordering and empowering you forthwith to repair to the house of Rossie Oliphant in the Aichills and there seize what horses and Arms etc you shall find fitt for his Majesties service and bring them to the toun of Perth to be employed that way'.[15] Additionally Mar also sent to Aberdeen for a printing press, 'types and utensills'.[16]

Arms surrenders give an idea of the sort of weapons that the Jacobites were carrying and in what proportions. In May 1717, at Banff, Aberdeenshire the surrenders after the Rising had netted a very large number of guns '691

8   Oates, *The Crucible of the Jacobite '15*, p.38; Rae, *A short history of the late rebellion*, p.188.
9   Pittock, *The Myth of the Jacobite Clans*, p.168.
10 Scott, *Memoirs of the insurrection in Scotland in 1715*, pp.99–100.
11 Szechi, *1715: The Great Jacobite Rebellion*, p.95.
12 B59/30/39 summons against rebels.
13 Pittock, *The Myth of the Jacobite Clans*, p.168; Allardyce, *Historical Papers Relating to the Jacobite Period, 1699–1750*, p.42.
14 Tayler and Tayler, *The Story of the Rising*, p.30.; Szechi, *1715: The Great Jacobite Rebellion*, p.110; Pittock, M, *The Myth of the Jacobite Clans*, p.169.
15 Kington-Oliphant, *The Jacobite Lairds*, p.33.
16 Allardyce, *Historical Papers Relating to the Jacobite Period, 1699–1750*, p.44.

guns and gunbarrells', and a further '360 pistols and pistol barrels'. There were also '1002 swords and sword blades', and in contrast to the image of the Jacobites with Lochaber axes – there were only 48 however significantly more than were around in 1745. Very few targes, only 20, these with the gun stocks were burnt.[17] Although General Wade, writing to the King in 1724, said that the Disarming Act of 1716 had 'been so ill executed that the clans most disaffected to your majesty's government [that is, the Jacobite clans] remain the best armed and consequently more of a capacity to be used as tools or instruments of any foreign power or domestic incendiary'.[18] The Lochaber axes mentioned here were generally a long, curved blade mounted on a shaft approximately two metres (just over six foot) topped with a hook. Many of the Jacobite foot soldiers in 1689 had carried them but as can be seen from the numbers in surrenders they were less common by 1715. Some men were seen about fully armed with guns, swords and dirks. 'John McArthur, servant to the Duke of Atholl, and armed with gun, sword and dirk did drink the Pretender's health with others in Kinross.'[19] In Perth in October 1716 12 firelocks – one without hammer or bayonet (only one is described as having a bayonet); four carabines and a fowling piece.[20] If the surrenders reflect the numbers of weapons in the field, the higher number of swords are reflected in accounts of the time which suggest the Jacobites had cutting weapons.

Cullen, in Moray about 13 miles from Banff in May of 1717, brought in 135 guns, nine gun barrels, nine Danish axes (lochabers), 234 swords and '74 pistols side and hulster'. Robert Low in Inverness had surrendered three guns, one pistol, 70 swords and an old fashioned two-handed sword which were valued at £1-10-8. While the year before Andrew Hay of Montblairy, the collector of Supply in Banffshire had made payments for 'ane gun, ane broadsword English mounting, ane other broad sword highland guard, ane small sword or rappier', Glenbuchat gave up 'a cache of 153 guns, 185 swords, 26 pistols and 19 targets'.[21]

Tullibardine took a shagreen (shark skin) cartridge box with him.[22] Patrick Grant, who was a gunsmith in Inverness surrendered four side pistols at £0-15-0.[23] Wade in 1724 suggested that 'great quantities of broken and useless arms were brought from Holland and delivered up those appointed to receive them at exorbitant prices'.

An English mounting such as the one from the weapons collected in Banffshire, on a sword from this period consisted of three vertical bars on either side; the knuckle guard and the secondary guard were connected by a pair of diagonal cross bars; the rearguards sloped steeply from the pommel

---

17 W. Crammond, *The Annals of Banff*, 2 vols (Aberdeen: New Spalding Club, 1891), p.118.

18 Allardyce, *Historical Papers Relating to the Jacobite Period, 1699–1750*, p.136.

19 B59/30/1 – complaints against persons.

20 B59/30/31 – weapons gathered.

21 Stewart-Murray and Anderson, *Chronicles of the Atholl and Tullibardine Families*, p.cviii.

22 M. Kelvin, *The Scottish Pistol: its history, design and manufacture* (London: Cygnus Arts; Madison: Fairleigh Dickinson University Press, 1996), p.188.

23 Crammond, *The Annals of Banff*, p.118; Pittock, *The Myth of the Jacobite Clans*, pp.168–9; M. Kelvin, *The Scottish Pistol: its history, design and manufacture* (London: Cygnus Arts; Madison: Fairleigh Dickinson University Press, 1996), p.188.

of the sword. A highland sword guard had a much larger rectangular plate decorated sometimes with hearts or occasionally a saltire cut out.[24] Possibly the best swords were made in Stirling, the blade of the sword was imported, often from Germany. Others came from the Netherlands and Spain, *Agus Spàinneach ann air ealchainn* (and Spanish swords on weapon racks). Some of the swords had engravings such as 'Prospertie to Schotland and No Union', showing the origin of the sword blade.[25] Many civilians, and therefore many Jacobites, carried a small sword which had no particular Scottish form. At this time all gentlemen were expected to carry a sword and know how to use it. The two-handed sword, which still came up occasionally in weapons surrenders was obsolete.

Many of the guns that the Jacobites were using had been imported, chiefly from the Netherlands[26] however those aside the pistols that many also had were made in Scotland.[27] The pistols were all a single shot type with a flintlock firing mechanism. The barrels were generally 10 to 14 inches (25.4 to 36 centimetres). The metal work of the earlier pistols, the sort that might have used at Killiecrankie and subsequent battles made engraving popular. The most popular shapes for the period with which we are concerned are the scroll butts or ramshorn, and at the start of the eighteenth century the heart shaped butts. They were flintlock pistols and these were often made in Scotland and some in the Highlands. Scottish pistols were made in pairs, and until around 1700 made with right and left hand locks.[28] The Highlanders are described as wearing them on their belts, with belt-hooks for hanging over the belt: 'they have a ponyard knife and fork in one sheath, hanging at one side of their Belt, their Pistol at the other and their Snuff-Mill before; with a great broad Sword by side';[29] 'At the battle of Sheriffmuir in 1715, it is reported that regarding the troops of the Earl of Mar the first line consisted of ten battalions of infantry, all clansmen in tartan, armed with claymore and dirk, pistols and target.'[30] Some of those taking part in the raid on Loch Lomond are described as:

> fourty or fifty stately fellows in their short hose and belted plaids, arm'd each of them with a well fixe'd gun on his shoulder, a shoulder, a strong handsome target with a sharp pointed steel of about half an ell in length, screw'd into the navel of

24 E. Oakeshott, *European Weapons and Armour: From the Renaissance to the Industrial Revolution* (Woodbridge: The Boydell Press, 2000), p.177. Lord Mungo Murray whose picture is in this book has a sword hilt that shows an early form of Highland guard often called a beaknose.
25 Pittock, *The Myth of Jacobite Clans*, p.165.
26 These guns were mostly made in Lowlands, Doune being the most famous place, but guns were also produced in Aberdeen, Brechin, Dundee, Edinburgh, Perth and Stirling, for example see Kelvin, *The Scottish Pistol*, p.162. There were however some manufactured in the Highlands: Mull, Glenelg and Inverness being some of the places in the north.
27 Kelvin, *The Scottish Pistol*, p.124. Contrary to the current appearance of many extant guns, the barrels were blued originally.
28 Kelvin, *The Scottish Pistol*, pp.104, 105, 114, 115, 123–8.
29 Stewart, *Old and Rare Scottish Tartans*, p.29.
30 Kelvin, *The Scottish Pistol*, p.93; Pittock, *The Myth of the Jacobite Clans*, p.165.

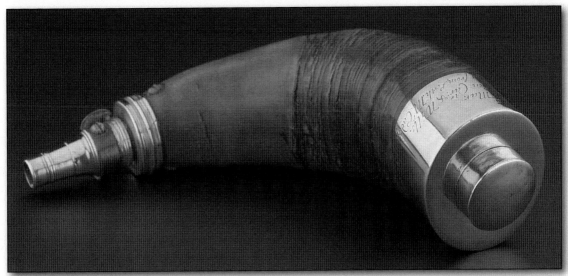

A ram's horn powder flask with silver mounts and an inscription about the Jacobite Rising in 1715 which reads 'Dumblain fight Nov 13 1715 / Kings Gen: D Argile, Pretenders & Mar / INvs: AtkDefd by Erl of SurInd: Prsin: Takn by Gen: Catr& Wills / Ye Pretender ye Erl of Mar & ye rest of ye party run away to Perth. Mr Cadogan ye Kings General: Gen: 30 Jan 1715/16.' The inscription also talks about fighting in the North of Scotland, the taking of Jacobite prisoners after the battle of Preston in England and finally the retreat of the Jacobites from Perth. (Image © National Museums Scotland)

it, on his left arm, a sturdy claymore by his side and a pistol or two with a durk and a knife on his belt.[31]

The Jacobites had 11 cannon at Sheriffmuir, six brass and five iron, four of these came from Dundee, the others from Dunottar.[32] Unfortunately, they did not have the powder and ball to use them properly and in common with the other Jacobite Risings they suffered from the lack of trained gunners. In January 1716, four cannon were sent to the Marquess of Huntly – 'two belonging to Alexander Scott, ship master weighting eighteen hundereth and four pounds weight and two belonging to the towne of Aberdeen weighting thirty six hundered three quarters of ane hundred and twenty two punds weight'. At Sheriffmuir the Government captured four cannon, quite possibly Dundee's demi-culverins, since they were returned to the city eventually, as well ammunition carts, baggage carts, 13 flags and the royal standard.[33] When the Jacobites abandoned Perth as the Rising fell apart, 18 iron and three brass cannon were thrown into the river.[34]

Although even in 1715, to judge from the arms surrenders, it does not appear that every man had a targe, they were obviously of more use to those in the front ranks than the men behind. Targes were carried in 1689, *The Grameid* is full of descriptions of men carrying targes – Macdonald of Keppoch 'from his shoulder hung the tartan plaid' and he carried a shield studded with brazen knobs. Lochiel carried a shield on his left arm.[35] A targe or target as it was often called at the time, was a small round shield

---

31 Quoted in Kelvin, *The Scottish Pistol*, p.93.
32 B59/30/46 Discharge.
33 Fletcher of Saltoun in his letters says, '5 cannon, some wagons with ammunition and 14 standards with colours'. I. Murray (ed.), 'Letters of Andrew Fletcher of Saltoun and his family, 1715–1716', in *Miscellany of the Scottish History Society. Volume X* (1965), p.151.
34 Allardyce, *Historical Papers Relating to the Jacobite Period, 1699–1750*), p.47; Oates, *The Crucible of the Jacobite '15*, p.127; SP 54/10/46A, an account of the engagement near Dunblain.
35 Murdoch and Philip, *The Grameid*, p.124.

A Highland targe or target made from wood, covered in leather with brass studs, with a double eagle in the centre, the symbol of the MacDonalds. (Image © National Museums Scotland)

about 20–27 inches (about 50–70cms) in diameter and weighing about 4.4–7.7lbs (2–3.5 kilos) depending on whether it had metal studs. Fletcher of Saltoun, writing in 1715, says that 'the outward forme of ane Highland Targe is a convex circle, about 2 foot diameter, but some have them oval; the innermost part of it nixt the man's breast is a skin with the hair upon it, which is only a cover to a steel plate, which is not very thick'.[36]

Not all targes at this time had a steel plate, many were just made from two very thin layers of flat wooden board with the grain of each layer of wood at right angles to one and other and then fixed together with wooden pegs. The plate has a handle which was fixed and 'hath two parts, one that the left arm passes throw till near the elbow, the other that the Hand lays hold on'. There is a cork plate which 'covers the Steel plate exactly, but betwixt the Cork and the Steel plate there is Wooll [sometimes straw] stuffed in very hard: the Cork is covered with plain well-wrought leather, which is nailed to the Cork with nails that have brass heads, in order round, drawing thicker towards the center.' Some targes had a central brass boss and others a steel spike which Saltoun calls a 'Stiletto (I know not the right name of it, but I call it so, because it is a sort of short poignard) which fixes into the Steel plate and wounds the Enemy when they close'. Exactly like the targes described in the Loch Lomond incident – 'strong handsome target with a sharp pointed steel of about half an ell in length, screw'd into the navel'; 'When not in use this spike could be unscrewed and placed in a sort of sheath at the back of the targe.[37]

Ther is a peece of Brass in the forme of a Cupelo about 3 inches over and coming halfway out on the Stiletto and is fixed upon it. Within this brass ther is a peece of Horn of the same forme like a cup, out of which they drink their usquebaugh [whisky], but it being pierced in the under part by the Stiletto, when they take it off to use it as a cup, they are obliged to apply the forepart of the end of their finger to the hole to stop it, so that they might drink out of their cup.

---

36 S. Maxwell, *The Highland Targe, The Scottish Art Review Vol IX No2* (Glasgow Art Gallery and Museums Association, 1963), pp.2–5.

37 I. Murray (ed.), 'Letters of Andrew Fletcher of Saltoun and his family, 1715–1716', in *Miscellany of the Scottish History Society. Volume X* (1965), p.151.

He goes on to claim that:

> The nails sometimes throw off a ball [that is a musket ball], especially when it hits the Targe asquint: but tho' a ball came directly upon it and miss the nail heads, piercing betwixt them, yet they reckon that the leather, the cork, the wooll so deaden the ball, that the Steel plate, tho' thin, repells it and lodges it in the wooll.[38]

Eighteenth century targes were generally decorated with concentric circles or a central brass boss which then had lesser bosses around it. There are a few exceptions to this such as the targe in Perth Museum and Art gallery which has stars on it. Seventeenth-century targes quite frequently have animal decoration, similar in style to that seen on contemporary highland brooches and well as interlacing designs.

---

38 Murray, *Letters of Andrew Fletcher of Saltoun*, in *Miscellany of the Scottish History Society. Volume X*, p.153.

6

Rebellious Highlanders

Ris an caintre Rob Ruadh-
'S math thig breacan mun cairt is claidhe dhuit
Mar rid ag a' chin noir
Air a chriosan bu bhoidhch'
Cha bu 'tais ann an tos Catha thu
(Rob Roy is what they called you –
You look good wearing a plaid and a sword
With a gold mounted pistol
On the finest of belts,
You were not soft in the front of battle)[1]

Earl Marischal, Marquess of Tullibardine, William Mackenzie, 5th Earl of
    Seaforth
Brigadier William Mackintosh of Borlum. Lord George Murray, Cameron
    of Locheil
Regiment Galicia from Spain, under its Colonel, Don Nicolás de Castro
    Bolaño
Clan Cameron,
Clan MacGregor – with Rob Roy MacGregor
Clan Mackinnon
Clan Mackenzie
Clan Murray
Clan Keith
Lidcoat's and other volunteers.[2]

It had been nearly 30 years since regular soldiers from a sympathetic
European power had landed in support of the Stuarts however, the amount
of support was not as much as had been hoped for. The Spanish Armada with
its 5,000 troops and 15,000 muskets had intended to land in the English West
Country where there were known to be Jacobites. The Cornish tin miners

---

1   Anon., *Marbhrann do Rob Roy Macgregor* (An elegy for Rob Roy Macgregor).
2   The name Lidcoat was used in a letter from Tullibardine to Mar on 16 June 1719. It probably
    refers to Glengarry.

The Battle of Glenshiel 1719, by Peter Tillemans. This depiction of the Battle of Glenshiel was based on contemporary descriptions and plans. The figure on the left on top of the hill holding a gun and a targe is probably Lord George Murray; he is wearing a blue bonnet and what appears to be a plaid and trews. On the opposite hill can be seen the Spanish regulars in their white coats with yellow cuffs. On the top of that hill, a figure is holding a sword, a targe and wearing trews – he is likely to be Rob Roy MacGregor. In the foreground on the right hand side, there is the government baggage train; there are some figures with the horse, two of whom appear to be women. Purchased with assistance from the National Heritage Memorial Fund & the Art Fund 1984. (Image © National Galleries of Scotland)

in particular were supposed to favour the Jacobite cause. The Spanish fleet, which was carrying about 13 regiments of foot and one regiment of dragoons hit a storm and was blown off course resulting in them losing supplies and some of the arms that they were bringing to support the Rising. The Scottish landing was intended simply to be a diversion, however due to the bad weather the two ships with approximately 300 Spanish soldiers and another 2,000 muskets were the only ones who landed. Five years after Glenshiel, General Wade complained that:

> The Spaniards who landed at Castle donnan in the year 1719 brought with them a great Number of arms, They were delivered to the Rebellious, Highlanders who are still possessed of them many of which I have seen in my passage through that Country and I judge them to the same from their peculiar make and the fashion of their locks.[3]

---

3   Allardyce, *Historical Papers Relating to the Jacobite Period, 1699–1750*), p.136.

In Scotland, Tullibardine and some of his fellow conspirators had been 'buying up a very considerable quantity of fire-arms, broad-swords, and targets from the Netherlands where swords could be bought at good prices. A Dutch arms dealer was arrested in April.[4] This is interesting as it appears to contradict the idea that none of the arms surrenders post the 1715 were real and that as Wade implied everything that had been given in were 'broken and useless arms' since if that had been the case then it would seem likely that Tullibardine and the others would have had considerable numbers of weapons ready to give to those that did rise in Scotland. The Earl of Seaforth brought to the agreed rendezvous on Lewis 'a quantity of aminition'.[5] 'The latest intelligence was that the Earl of Seaforth with several hundred foreigners had landed on the Isle of Lewis', written in a letter dated the 5 April 1719.[6]

> The fleets being dispers'd, there was no way of preserveing it in ane open place; upon which the Castle of Islean donan being visited, it was found by putting it there with a small guaird the old walls and vaults would be sufficient to keep it from any flying party by land, or attaque by sea. Accordingly, it was put there in the best manner with all the dilligence the dificultys they had to struggle with could permitt, and Capt. Stapletone with a Spainish Lieutennent and above 40 souldiers were sent to garison the place.[7]

However, Royal Navy warships arrived in Loch Alsh. On the evening of 10 May they bombarded Eilean Donan Castle, where most of the Jacobite provisions and ammunition were stored. After three days of relatively little success through this method of attack, Captain Herdman of the *Enterprise*, one of the warships, launched an assault on the castle, overwhelming the defenders and leaving them little option but to surrender both themselves and their weapons, which consisted of 343 barrels of powder and 52 barrels of musket balls. 'On the 10th in the morning the three ships came up, and anchor'd within musquet shot of the Castle. They were no sooner moor'd than they begun to fire on the place, which continued the whole day, but the walls being very thick they could not make a breach.'[8]

In the contemporary painting of the battle of Glenshiel by Peter Tillemans which is based on accounts from eyewitnesses, the Spanish regulars, approximately 200 of who were actually on the field since some had been taken prisoner with the ammunition and others were guarding the baggage; are wearing white coats with yellow cuffs, their cocked hats appear to be decorated with white lace although in general the officers would have had silver lace. Intriguingly though the same letter which says that Seaforth has landed with 'several hundred foreigners' also said 'Upon Sunday the 5th of

---

4   J. Worton, *The Battle of Glenshiel: The Jacobite Rising in 1719* (Warwick: Helion & Company, 2018), p.115.

5   Kington-Oliphant, *The Jacobite lairds of Gask*, p.452.

6   SP 55/9/71 – a copy of a letter from George Monroe of Culrain dated 1719. I am indebted to Andrew Mckenzie for finding this reference for me.

7   Kington-Oliphant, *The Jacobite lairds of Gask*, pp.452–3.

8   Kington-Oliphant, *The Jacobite lairds of Gask*, pp.452–3.

April the late E Seaforth landed from the Lewis with a great many Gentlemen, and 800 forreigners (whose livery is blue & white) at Polow in Garloch.' It goes on to say that 400 of this seemingly much larger force marched by land to Kintail and the reminder to Stankhouse in Gairloch.[9]

In the painting it can be seen that despite the defensive nature of the Jacobite engagement some have discarded their guns and are using swords. There was additionally no highland charge during this battle; almost all of the fighting was done with guns. If the number of muskets given are accurate then there would have been more guns than men and even allowing for the depreciation of powder and ammunition caused by the loss of the stores in the previous month then every Jacobite should have had a gun. Most likely a Spanish one – which would have been a flintlock, very similar to the model 1717 fusil produced by the French at this time however Spanish gunsmiths commonly mounted the main spring on the inside of lock [this may be why Wade thought they looked different to the other firelocks he was used to seeing].[10] The characteristics that make a Spanish flintlock are the horizontal sears [that is the part of the trigger mechanism that holds the hammer until enough pressure has been applied to shoot the gun] – meaning that the full cock and half cock sears go through the lockplate at a right angle.[11] The most clearly recognisable features are the big externally mounted mainspring and the large ring of the top jaw screw. It is of course possible that some of the Dutch imports bought by Tullibardine were also Spanish guns. The Netherlands being the arms market of choice at this time. The men taking part in the 1719 Rising obviously looked very similar to those in 1715. They did however look different to the Jacobites of 1689. One of the keys ways was the lack of facial hair. By the turn of the eighteenth century most men were clean shaven. It was probably one of the few times in relatively recent western European history when virtually all men were beardless. Therefore, it can be said with some confidence that the men who fought at Sherrifmuir, Preston and Glenshiel would not have beards or moustaches.

Sir Walter Scott had some of Rob Roy's relics including a flint lock gun with a long barrel [four foot long or 1.2m approximately which makes it longer than a French fusil from this time] 'an old flintlock gun of extreme length, with a silver plate containing the initials RMC' as one Edwardian travel writer described it.[12] This is supposedly the same gun with which his son, Robin Oig shot John Maclaren of Invernenty. It has an octagonal barrel, the stock has an engraved brass plate and another plate on top decorated with shell pattern. The trigger guard is brass also. The stock is 17 inches [43.18cm], it also has three inlaid silver bands which are generally [although not always

---

9   This is much larger number than the other accounts say. If he is mistaken about that – and it seems likely he is since otherwise there was an unaccounted troop of Spaniards somewhere in the hills near Kintail for some time – then could he have got the livery wrong? SP 55/9/71 – a copy of a letter from George Monroe of Culrain dated 1719.

10   J. Lavin, *The History of Spanish Firearms* (New York: Arco Pub Co., 1963), p.200. The muskets used by the Jacobites would, like all early eighteenth-century guns, have had a wooden ramrod often referred to as a scouring stick.

11   Lavin, *The History of Spanish Firearms*, pp.167, 184, 210.

12   C. Olcott, *The Country of Sir Walter Scott* (London: Cassell, 1913), p.185.

in silver] characteristic of the slightly later guns produced in 1720s and 30s and not those that might have been used in 1719. Also an 'old highland broadsword', with Andrea Ferrara blade and a basket hilt. On each side of the blade it has the name Andrea Ferrara with three orbs and crosses [given that Rob Roy is depicted in the painting of Glenshiel with a sword in hand it is not unreasonable to think this might be the one he is holding].

There is also a sporran associated Rob Roy with four concealed pistols in it that would fire if the sporran was not opened correctly, which is in the National Museum of Scotland. Sir Walter in his novel about Rob Roy says, in a passage clearly inspired by this sporran (which he described as being made from the skin of sea otter), 'I advise no man to attempt opening this sporran until he has my secret … and then twisting one button in one direction, another in another, pulling one stud upward and pressing another downward, the mouth of the purse opened a small steel pistol was concealed within the purse, the trigger of which was connected with the mounting, and made part of the machinery, so that the weapon would certainly be discharged.'

Given that some six years later Rob Roy is surrendering 20 guns, 21 broadswords, three targes, five dirks and one pistol,[13] it possible to feel that some of General Wade's feelings about the Highlands being awash with Spanish guns are justified. Although a generation later James's son Charles Edward Stuart was to find a paucity of weapons a problem again, so presumably these guns had all disappeared in the intervening years.

The failure of the 1719 Rising meant that it would be another 25 years before there would be another attempt at Rising in support of the Stuarts.

---

13   Stevenson, *The Hunt for Rob Roy*, p.135.

Colour Plate Commentaries

Plate 1

Highland Chief, 1715
He is wearing a knitted blue bonnet, which might have had a white cockade on it since they were worn in the 1715 Rising. His hair is long, as was common in Highland culture. His jacket or doublet is made from a tartan that has red in the sett, as would be expected from a tartan worn by an elite man. He also has a simple sporran or purse and a targe. As a man of some importance then, he would have carried a basket hilted broadsword, two pistols (they virtually always came in pairs) and a musket. The wearing of tartan and highland clothes was embraced by many after the union of 1707 as a political statement, and a sign of their commitment to the House of Stuart.

Highland Man, 1689
He has a knitted, blue bonnet, worn flat on his head. Martin says that the bonnets were 'some blue, some black and some grey'. Perhaps fortunately this Highlander has not discarded his plaid, as some men did when about to fight, running towards the enemy with their swords or Lochaber axes at the ready. He is carrying a Lochaber axe which many of the poorer men carried in both 1689 and 1715.

Plate 2

Trooper, the Royal Regiment of Scots horse 1689
One of Dundee's troopers, the Royal Regiment of Scots horse 1689. One of the 50 men who stayed loyal to Viscount Dundee after William and Mary came to the throne and Dundee raised the standard for King James. They wore red coats with brass buttons, lined and faced in yellow. They had uncocked black hats with a yellow hat band which is likely to have been edged in yellow tape. They wore over-knee riding boots and buff coloured breeches.

Lowland Officer 1689
This particular officer is dressed in Lowland fashion as Dundee, Cannon and Buchan would have been for the campaign. He has kept his scarlet coat with

gold lace. His hat would have been made from beaver with white feathers, officers also wore crimson scarves or sashes. This officer, as Dundee did, is wearing half armour.

Plate 3

Lowland Levy, 1715

Not every man who came out in the '15 was wearing Highland clothes or tartan. This man is wearing a coat of sheep's colour fabric with wool buttons like those from the coat found on the Barrock estate, something typical of many plebeian coats. He is wearing blue knitted stockings, probably hand knitted in Aberdeenshire, and breeches also made from undyed wool fabric. He would have been wearing a waistcoat under his coat. He has a long gun. Scottish long guns, like Scots pistols never had trigger guards. Most Scottish long guns had wooden stocks, however occasionally they were made entirely of metal like the pistols.

Plate 4

Spanish infantryman, 1719

A Spaniard from Glenshiel, 1719. He is a regular soldier, one of the 300 men from the Regiment Galicia from Spain, under its Colonel, Don Nicolás de Castro Bolaño, in his white wool coat with yellow cuffs, although there is one report of the foreigners 'whose livery is blue and white'. His cocked hat has white lace and he is wearing white stockings. He is carrying a Spanish musket and a hanger.

Plate 5

Flag of the Appin Stewarts

Blue silk with a yellow saltire. The Appin Stewarts are described in *The Grameid* as carrying blue banners. Lieutenant Colt after Killiecrankie said, that 'he saw a young man who wes said to be Stewart of Appine, and that ho had about a hundred and thretty men or therby of his own in armes with him, and join'd the Viscount of Dundee, in ther march fiom Lochabber to Badenoch, and that they had collours, and wer in good order.'

The Lion Rampant – the Royal Standard

The flag that Dundee raised on Dudhope Law to begin the Rising was most likely the lion rampant. Philip described a 'signa Caledoniis Rege – standard of the Scottish kings'. He also referred it elsewhere to the 'tawny lion'. Philip carried it himself when Dundee began the campaign. '*Regia et ipse meis portabam signa lacertis*' ('And I myself was bearing in my arms the royal standard').

Plate 6

Flag of Nicholas Purcell's Regiment and the Flag of Cameron of Lochiel

The red saltire on a white ground of St Patrick was carried by the Irish Nicholas Purcell's regiment at Killiecrankie. Philip, in *The Grameid*, mentioned that the Camerons had a red flag. This one has Lochiel's own coat of arms.

Plate 7

Flag of Spalding of Glenkilry and the Thistle Banner

The banner of Andrew Spalding of Glenkilry in Perthshire is said to have been carried in the Jacobite Risings of 1715 and 1745. The banner bears the coat of arms of the Spaldings of Glenkilry, with the motto NOBILI SERVITIUM, and the initials A.S. It is still extant.

This flag, known as the 'Thistle banner', has a central crowned thistle and the motto NEMO ME IMPUNE LACESSET (No-one shall hurt me with impunity). In one corner is a blue saltire, in the other three, thistles. The flag is dated 1716 and may have been one of the flags carried by Mar.

Plate 8

The green banner of Clan Macpherson and the arms of the Duke of Gordon as carried by the Gordons of Strathavan

The green banner of Clan Macpherson, The Macphersons were out in both under Dundee and in '15. It was said that no battle in which they ever carried this banner was lost (presumably it wasn't at Sherrifmuir). There is a copy of the banner in the Clan Macpherson Museum.

The Gordons of Strathavan carried a flag with the arms of the Duke of Gordon during the 1715 Rising. There may have been a ducal coronet (or crown) placed above the arms signifying the title of Duke, granted in 1684.

Bibliography

Primary Sources

National Archives
GD44/51/167/4
SP 54/10/46A
SP 35/1/f30
SP 54/3/31
SP 54/10/45A

Perth & Kinross Archives
B59/30/4
B59/30/34
B59/30/36
B59/30/31
B59/30/39

Weekly Journal or British Gazetteer 26/11/1715

The Post Boy 23/07/1713. 24/09/1713

Flying Post or The Post Master 11/06/1715

Printed Primary Sources

Allardyce, J. (ed.), *Historical Papers Relating to the Jacobite Period, 1699–1750*, 2 vols (Aberdeen: 1895, 1896)

Anon., *Postscript to the St. Jamess [sic] post. Being a supplement to the paper of this day. no. 133. Monday, Nov. 28.* (1715). *This day arriv'd a mail from Scotland. Edinburgh, Nov. 22*

Anon., *The Loch Lomond Expedition with some short reflections on the Perth Manifesto* (Glasgow, 1715)

Anon., *An Historical Account of the Highlanders: describing their country, division into clans ... set forth in a view of the rebellion in Scotland* (Dublin, 1715)

Anon., *The exercise of the foot with the evolutions, according to the words of command, as they are explained : as also the forming of battalions, with directions to be observed by all colonels, captains and other officers in His Majesties armies. Likewise, the exercise of the dragoons both on horse-back and foot. With the rules of war in the day of battel, when encountering the enemy, ordered by Sir Thomas Livingston, Major General, and commander in chief of their Majesties forces in Scotland. Recommended to all (officers as well as souldiers) in their Majesties armies* (Edinburgh: 1693)

Stewart-Murray, J.J.J.H., Duke of Atholl, and Anderson, J., *Chronicles of the Atholl and Tullibardine Families* (Edinburgh: privately printed, 1908)

Balfour-Melville, E.W.M., *An Account of the Proceedings of the Estates in Scotland, 1689–1690* (Edinburgh: Scottish History Society, 1954)

Burt, E., ed. Simmons, A., *Burt's Letters from the North of Scotland* (Edinburgh: Birlinn, 1998. First published 1754)

Calamy, E., ed. Rutt, J.T., *An Historical Account Of My Own Life, With Some Reflections On the Times I Have Lived In* (London: H. Colburn and R. Bentley, 1829)

Campbell, Lord Archibald, *Records of Argyll: Legends, traditions, and recollections of Argyllshire Highlanders* (Edinburgh: W. Blackwood, 1885)

Chambers, R., *Domestic Annals of Scotland, from the Revolution to the Rebellion of 1745*, vol. II (Edinburgh: W. & R. Chambers, 1860)

Crammond, W., *The Annals of Banff*, 2 vols (Aberdeen: New Spalding Club, 1891)

Dalyell, J., and Beveridge, J., 'Inventory of the Plenishing of the House of the Binns at the Date of the Death of General Thomas Dalyell, 21st August 1683. Edited from the Original Documents in the Family Records', *Proceedings of the Society of Antiquaries of Scotland* 58 (1924)

Dodds, James, *The Diary and General Expenditure Book of William Cunningham of Craigends ... Kept Chiefly from 1673 to 1680* (Edinburgh: printed at the University Press by T. and A. Constable for the Scottish History Society, 1887)

Dunton, J., *The Night-walker: Or, Evening Rambles in Search after Lewd Women, with the Conferences Held with Them, &c.* (London, 1696)

Gregory, Donald, and the Iona Club (eds), *Collectanea de Rebus Albanicis, Consisting of Original Papers and Documents Relating to the History of the Highlands and Islands of Scotland* (Edinburgh: T.G. Stevenson, 1847)

Hallen, A.W.C., *The Account Book of Sir John Foulis of Ravelston, 1671–1707* (Edinburgh: printed at the University Press by T. and A. Constable for the Scottish History Society, 1894)

Henshall, A., 'Clothing found at Hunstgarth, Harray, Orkney', *Proceedings of the Society of Antiquaries of Scotland*, 101 (1969)

Kington-Oliphant, T. L., *The Jacobite Lairds of Gask* (London, Published for the Grampian Club by C. Griffin & Co., 1870)

Loveday, J., *Diary of a tour in 1732 through parts of England, Wales, Ireland and Scotland* (Edinburgh: privately printed, 1890)

Mackay, W. (ed.), *The Letter-Book of Bailie John Steuart of Inverness 1715–1752* (Edinburgh: University Press, 1915)

Mackay, H., Maitland Hog, J., Fraser Tyler, P. and Urquhart, A., *Memoirs of the War Carried on in Scotland and Ireland, M.DC.LXXXIX.–M.DC.XCI: with an appendix of original papers* (Edinburgh: Maitland Club, 1833)

Mackay, J., and Bannatyne Club, *The Life of Lieut.-General Hugh Mackay of Scoury, Commander in Chief of the Forces in Scotland, 1689 and 1690...* (Edinburgh: Laing and Forbes, 1836)

MacLeod, R.C., *The Book of Dunvegan. Being Documents from the Muniment Room of the MacLeods of MacLeod at Dunvegan Castle, Isle of Skye* (Aberdeen: Printed for the Third Spalding Club, 1938)

Martin, M.A., *A Description of the Western Islands of Scotland, circa 1695* (Edinburgh: Birlinn, 1994)

MacConechy, J., *Papers Illustrative of the Political Condition of the Highlands of Scotland from the Year M.DC.LXXXIX to M.DC.XCVI* (Glasgow: Maitland Club, 1845)

Millar, A.H., *A Selection of Scottish Forfeited Estates Papers: 1715; 1745* (Edinburgh: Printed at the University Press by T. and A. Constable for the Scottish History Society, 1909)

Morer, T., *A Short Account of Scotland. Being a Description of the Nature of that Kingdom, and what the Constitution of it is in Church and State* (1702). ECCO, accessed 17 March 2019

Murdoch, A.D., and Philip. J., *The Grameid: An Heroic Poem Descriptive of the Campaign of Viscount Dundee in 1689, and Other Pieces* (Edinburgh: Printed at the University Press by T. and A. Constable for the Scottish History Society, 1888)

Murray, I. (ed.), 'Letters of Andrew Fletcher of Saltoun and his family, 1715–1716', in *Miscellany of the Scottish History Society.*, vol. X (Edinburgh: Scottish History Society, 1965)

Ormonde, J.B., and Dickson. W., *The Jacobite Attempt of 1719: Letters of James Butler, Second Duke of Ormonde, Relating to Cardinal Alberoni's Project for the Invasion of Great Britain on Behalf of the Stuarts, and to the Landing of a Spanish Expedition in Scotland* (Edinburgh: University Press, 1895).

Rae, P., *A short history of the late rebellion and of the conduct of divine Providence ... : in a letter from Edinburgh to a gentleman at Dumfries* (Edinburgh: Printed by Robert Brown, 1716)

Ramsay, A., *Tartana: or, the Plaid* [1718], ECCO, accessed 1 February 2019

Scott, W. (ed), *Memoirs of the insurrection in Scotland in 1715* (Edinburgh, 1845)

Scott, W.R., *The Records of a Scottish Cloth Manufactory at New Mills, Haddingtonshire, 1681–1703* (Edinburgh: Scottish History Society, 1905)

Scott-Moncrieff, R. (ed.), *The Household Book of Lady Grisell Baillie, 1692–1733* (Edinburgh: Printed at the University Press by T. and A. Constable for the Scottish History Society, 1911)

Smythe, G., *Letters of John Grahame of Claverhouse, Viscount of Dundee, with Illustrative Documents* (Edinburgh: J. Bannatyne, 1826)

Story, T., *A Journal Of The Life Of Thomas Story* (Newcastle upon Tyne: Printed by Isaac Thompson and Company, 1747)

Taylor, J., *A Journey to Edenborough in Scotland* (Edinburgh, 1903)

Printed Secondary Sources

Bennett, H., 'A Murder Victim Discovered: Clothing and Other Finds from an Early Eighteenth-Century Grave on Arnish Moor, Lewis', *Proceedings of the Society of Antiquaries of Scotland*, 106 (1974–5)

Black, R. (ed.), *An Lasair, Anthology of Eighteenth-Century Scottish Gaelic Verse* (Edinburgh: Birlinn, 2001)

Blackmore, D., *Destructive and Formidable: British Infantry Firepower 1642–1765* (London: Frontline Books, 2014)

Brown, I. (ed.), *From Tartan to Tartanry, Scottish Culture, History and Myth* (Edinburgh: Edinburgh University Press, 2010)

Burnett, J., Mercer, K., and Quye, A., 'The Practice of Dyeing Wool in Scotland *c*. 1790– *c*.1840', *Folk Life*, 42:1 (2003)

Butt, J., and Ponting, K. (eds.), *Scottish Textile History* (Aberdeen: Aberdeen University Press, 1987)

Capwell, T., *The Real Fighting Stuff: Arms and Armour at Glasgow Museums* (Glasgow, Glasgow City Council (Museums), 2007)

Cheape, H., and Grant, I.F., *Periods In Highland History*, 3rd edition (New York: Barnes & Noble, 2000)

Cheape, H., *Tartan: The Highland Habit*, 3rd edition (Edinburgh, National Museums of Scotland, 2006)

Cheape, H., 'The Piper to the Laird of Grant', *Proceedings of the Society of Antiquaries of Scotland*, vol. 125 (1996)

Cheape, H., 'Gheibhte breacain charnaid ('Scarlet Tartans Would be Got …'): the Re-invention of Tradition'; in I. Brown (ed.), *From Tartan to Tartanry: Scottish Culture, History and Myth* (Edinburgh: Edinburgh University Press, 2012)

Clarke, B., 'Clothing the Family of an MP in the 1690s: An Analysis of the Day Book of Edward Clarke of Chipley, Somerset', *Costume*, 43 (2009)

Clyde, R., *From Rebel to Hero: The Image of the Highlander 1745–1830* (East Linton: Tuckwell, 1998)

Cormack, A. 'Some Remarks on The Provision of Cavalry Swords To the Georgian Army', *Journal of the Society for Army Historical Research*, vol. 93, no. 376 (2015)

Corp, E., *The King Over the Water: Portraits of the Stuarts in Exile after 1689* (Edinburgh: Scottish National Portrait Gallery, 2001)

Cunnington, P., and Willet, C., *The History of Underclothes* (London: Michael Joseph, 1951)

Dalton, C., *The Scots Army 1661–88* (London: Eyre & Spottiswoode, 1909)

Donaldson, W., *The Jacobite Song: Political Myth and National Identity* (Aberdeen: Aberdeen University Press, 1988)

Dunbar, J.T., *History of Highland Dress* (London: Batsford, 1962)

Dunbar, J.T., *The Costume of Scotland* (London: Batsford, 1989)

Ede-Borrett, S., *The Army of James II 1685–1688: The Birth of the British Army* (Solihull: Helion & Co., 2017)

Ellestad, C.D., 'The Mutinies of 1689', *Journal of the Society for Army Historical Research*, vol. 53, no. 213 (1975)

Faiers, J., *Tartan* (Oxford: Berg, 2008)

Fforde, C.A., *A Summer in Lochaber: The Jacobite Rising of 1689* (Isle of Colonsay: House of Lochar, 2002)

Gillies, A.L., *Songs of Gaelic Scotland* (Edinburgh: Birlinn, 2010)

Grant, I.F., and Cheape, H., *Periods in Highland History* (London: Shepheard-Walwyn, 1987)

Grant, K., "'And in Every Hamlet a Poet": Gaelic Oral Tradition and Postmedieval Archaeology in Scotland', *Historical Archaeology*, 48, no. 1 (2014)

Gulvin, C., *The Scottish Hosiery and Knitwear Industry 1680–1980* (Edinburgh: Donald, 1984)

Guthrie, Neil, *The Material Culture of the Jacobites* (Cambridge: Cambridge University Press, 2013)

Hart, A., and North, S., *Seventeenth- and Eighteenth-Century Fashion in Detail* (London: V&A Publishing, 2009)

Henshall, A., Seaby, W., Lucas, A., Smith, A., & Connor, A., 'The Dungiven Costume', *Ulster Journal of Archaeology*, 24/25 (1961)

Hill, J.M., *Celtic Warfare 1595–1793* (1986)

Hill, J.M., 'Killiecrankie and the Evolution of Highland Warfare', *War in History*, vol. 1, no. 2 (1994)

Holden, R.M.. 'The First Highland Regiment: the Argyllshire Highlanders', *The Scottish Historical Review*, vol. 3, no. 9 (1905)

Hume-Brown, P. (ed.), *Early Travellers in Scotland* (Edinburgh: D. Douglas, 1891)

Hynes, A. 'True Religion, Faith and the Jacobite Movement', in *Bonnie Prince Charlie and the Jacobites*, ed. D. Forsyth (Edinburgh: National Museums Scotland, 2017)

Kelvin, M., *The Scottish Pistol: its history, design and manufacture* (London: Cygnus Arts; Madison: Fairleigh Dickinson University Press,1996)

Lambert, M., 'Bespoke Versus Ready-Made: The Work of the Tailor in Eighteenth Century Britain', *Costume*, 44 (2010)

Lavin, J., *The History of Spanish Firearms* (New York: Arco Pub Co., 1963)

Lemire, B., 'The Theft of Clothes and Popular Consumerism in Early Modern England', *Journal of Social History*, 24:2 (1990)

Legon, E., 'Bound up with Meaning: The Politics and Memory of Ribbon Wearing in Restoration England and Scotland', *Journal of British Studies*, 56 (2017)

Lindsay, Colin, Earl of Balcarres, *Memoirs Touching the Revolution in Scotland* (Edinburgh: Bannatyne Club, 1841)

Lyndon, Brian, 'Military Dress and Uniformity 1680–1720', *Journal of the Society for Army Historical Research*, vol. 54, no. 218 (1976)

Linney-Drouet, C.A., 'British military dress from contemporary newspapers, 1682–1799: Extracts from the notebook of the late Revd Percy Sumner', *Journal of the Society for Army Historical Research*, vol. 78, no. 314 (2000)

MacDonald, P., *The 1819 Key Pattern Book: One Hundred Original Tartans* (Perth, Scotland: Jamieson & Munro, 1995)

Mackilliop, A., *More Fruitful than the Soil: Army, Empire and the Scottish Highlands 1715–1815* (East Linton: Tuckwell, 2000)

Maclean, J.A., 'The Sources, particularly the Celtic Sources, for the History of the Highlands in the Seventeenth Century' (1939), Unpublished PhD thesis

MacLeod, A. (ed.), *The Songs of Duncan Ban Macintyre* (Edinburgh: the Scottish Gaelic Texts Society, 1952)

MacKenzie, A. (ed), *Orain Iain Luim, Songs of John, Bard of Keppoch* (Edinburgh: Published by the Scottish Academic Press for the Scottish Gaelic Texts Society, 1973)

Marwick, W.H., 'Shops in Eighteenth- and Nineteenth-Century Edinburgh', *Book of the Old Edinburgh Club*, 30 (1959)

Maxwell, S., 'The Highland Targe', *The Scottish Art Review* Vol IX No.2 (Glasgow Art Gallery and Museums Association, 1963)

Mickel, L, "'Our Hielandmen": Scots in Court Entertainments at Home and Abroad 1507–1616', *Journal for the Society of Renaissance Studies* (2018)

Millar, A.H., 'Killiecrankie Described by an Eye-Witness', *The Scottish Historical Review*, vol. 3, no. 9, (1905)

Monod, P., *Jacobitism and the English People 1688–1788* (Cambridge: Cambridge University Press, 1993)

Nenadic, S., *Lairds and Luxury: The Highland Gentry in Eighteenth-Century Scotland* (Edinburgh: John Donald, 2007)

Nenadic,S, 'The Highlands of Scotland in the First Half of the Eighteenth Century: Consuming at a Distance', *British Journal for Eighteenth-Century Studies*, 28 (2005)

Nenadic, S., 'Middle-Rank Consumers and Domestic Culture in Edinburgh and Glasgow 1720–1840', *Past and Present*, 145:1 (1994)

Nenadic, S., 'Necessities: Food and Clothing in the Long Eighteenth Century', in Foyster, E., and Whatley, C.A. (eds.), *A History of Everyday Life in Scotland, 1600–1800* (Edinburgh: Edinburgh University Press, 2010)

Oakeshott, E., *European Weapons and Armour: From the Renaissance to the Industrial Revolution* (Woodbridge: The Boydell Press, 2000)

Oates, J., *The Crucible of the Jacobite '15 – The Battle of Sheriffmuir 1715* (Solihull: Helion & Company, 2017)

Oates, J., *The Battle of Killiecrankie, The First Jacobite Campaign 1689–1691* (Warwick: Helion & Company, 2018)

Partington, W. (ed.), *The Private Letter Book of Sir Walter Scott* (London: Hodder & Stoughton, 1930)

Pentland, G., '"We Speak for the Ready": Images of Scots in Political Prints, 1707–1832', *The Scottish Historical Review*, vol. 90, No. 229, Part 1 (April 2011)

Pittock, M., *The Myth of the Jacobite Clans* (Edinburgh: Edinburgh University Press, 2015)

Pittock, M., *Material Culture and Sedition, 1688–1760: Treacherous Objects, Secret Places* (Basingstoke: Palgrave Macmillan, 2013)

Quinton, R., *Glasgow Museums – Seventeenth Century Costume* (London: Unicorn Press, 2013)

Quye, A., and Cheape, H., 'Rediscovering the Arisaid', *Costume*, 42 (2008)

Quye, A., and Cheape, H., Burnett, J., Ferreira, E., Hulme, A., & McNab, H., 'An historical and analytical study of red, pink, green and yellow colours in quality 18th and early 19th century Scottish tartans', *Dyes in History & Archaeology*, 19 (2003)

Rawson, H., Burnett, J., and Quye, A., 'The Import of Textile Dyes to Scotland: The Case of William Wilson and Son, Tartan Weavers of Bannockburn, 1780–1820', *Review of Scottish Culture*, 13 (2000–2001)

Reid, S., *The Flintlock Musket, Brown Bess and Charleville 1715–1865* (Oxford: Osprey Publishing, 2016)

Robertson, J., *The First Highlander: Major-general David Stewart of Garth CB, 1768–1829* (East Linton: Tuckwell, 1998)

Rogers, Nicholas, 'Popular Protest in Early Hanoverian London', *Past and Present* No. 79 (May 1978)

Scarlett, J., 'Tartan: the Highland Cloth and Highland Art Form', in Butt, J., and Ponting, K. (eds.), *Scottish Textile History* (Aberdeen: Aberdeen University Press, 1987)

Scobie, I.H.M., 'The Scottish Tartan Manufacturers and Bonnet Makers', *Journal of the Society for Army Historical Research*, 21:82 (1942)

Scouller, R.E., 'Catholic and Jacobite Officers', *Journal of the Society for Army Historical Research*, vol. 65, no. 261 (1987)

Spufford, M., *The Great Reclothing of Rural England: Petty Chapmen and Their Wares in the Seventeenth Century* (London: Hambledon Press, 1984)

Stewart, D., *Old and Rare Scottish Tartans* (Edinburgh, 1893)

Stevenson, D., *The Hunt for Rob Roy: The Man and the Myths* (Edinburgh: Birlinn, 2016)

Stroh, S., 'The Modern Nation-State and Its Others: Civilizing Missions at Home and Abroad, Ca. 1600 to 1800', *In Gaelic Scotland in the Colonial Imagination: Anglophone Writing from 1600 to 1900*, (2017)

Styles, J., 'Clothing the North: The Supply of Non-Elite Clothing in the Eighteenth Century North of England', *Textile History*, 25:2 (1994)

Styles, J., *The Dress of the People: Everyday Fashion in Eighteenth-Century England* (New Haven: Yale University Press, 2007)

Szechi, D., *1715: The Great Jacobite Rebellion* (New Haven: Yale University Press, 2006)

Szechi, D., *The Jacobites: Britain and Europe, 1688–1788*, 2nd Edition (Manchester: Manchester University Press, 2019)

Tayler, A, and Tayler, H., *1715: The Story of the Rising* (London, New York: T. Nelson, 1936)

Tayler, A, and Tayler, H., 'Lord Forfar and the Fifteen', *Journal of the Society for Army Historical Research*, vol. 15, no. 59 (1936)

Taylor, E., 'Personality in Fashion: Case Studies of Localism in Eighteenth-century Scotland', *Fashion Practice*, 10:2 (2018)

Tuckett, S., 'Weaving the Nation: Scottish Clothing and Textile Cultures in the Long Eighteenth Century' (2010), unpublished PhD thesis

Watson, J. Carmichael, *Gaelic Songs of Mary MacLeod* (London: Blackie & Son, 1934)

Watt, Douglas. '"The laberinth of thir difficulties": the Influence of Debt on the Highland Elite *c.* 1550 – 1700', *The Scottish Historical Review*, vol. 85 no. 1 (2006)

Weatherill, L., 'Consumer Behaviour, Textiles and Dress in the Late Seventeenth and Early Eighteenth Centuries', *Textile History*, 22:2 (1991)

Whatley, C.A. "'Reformed Religion, Regime Change, Scottish Whigs and the Struggle for the "Soul" of Scotland', *c*. 1688–*c*. 1788', *The Scottish Historical Review*, 92, no. 233 (2013)

Wilcox, D., 'Scottish Late Seventeenth-Century Male Clothing: Some Context for the Barrock Estate Finds', *Costume*, vol. 50, no 2 (2016)

Wilcox, D., 'Scottish Late Seventeenth-Century Male Clothing (Part 2): The Barrock Estate Clothing Finds Described', *Costume*, vol. 51, Issue 1, March (2017)

Worton, J., *The Battle of Glenshiel, The Jacobite Rising in 1719* (Warwick: Helion & Company, 2018)